AWAKEN

SOUNDING THE ALARM ON SLEEPY CHRISTIANITY

DR. SCOTT WILSON

Awaken
Sounding the Alarm on Sleepy Christianity

by

Dr. Scott Wilson

Copyright © 2021

ISBN: 978-0-9903591-2-8

Independently Published

First Edition

All Scripture quotations are from the King James Version.

All rights reserved. No part of this publication may be reproduced or transmitted in any form or by any means, electronic or mechanical, including photocopy, recording, or any information storage retrieval system, without permission in writing from the copyright owner.

Table of Contents

Chapter 1 – Knowing the Time 1

Chapter 2 – Spiritual Sleep 25

Chapter 3 – Slumbering Sinners 38

Chapter 4 – Snoozing Saints........................... 56

Chapter 5 – Wake Up Call.............................. 77

Chapter 6 – Blow the Trumpet 92

Chapter 7 – Waking Up 113

Chapter 8 – Don't Hit the Snooze Button 142

Chapter 9 – The Awakened Church 166

Chapter 10 – See the Fields 200

About the Author 223

1

Knowing the Time

And that, knowing the time, that now it is high time to awake out of sleep: for now is our salvation nearer than when we believed. – **Romans 13:11**

When I met my wife, she had been a public-school teacher for almost five years, and she continued to teach for the first five years of our marriage. I remembered school from the student perspective but being married to a teacher opened my eyes to a side of education that I didn't even know existed. School has changed so much since I was a student, and it was hard for me to comprehend

Chapter 1 – Knowing the Time

the changing environment and attitudes of both the administration and the student body. The stories my wife told me about her job sounded more like the experiences of a prison guard rather than a high school teacher. Even though many of the students were challenging, my wife was very fortunate because she mainly taught level two and three honors classes. She was blessed to be able to teach students who were interested in the subject and who had a desire to learn. These students were destined for a college education and to take future leadership roles in our society.

My wife taught Spanish, and part of her curriculum was to teach her students how to tell someone the time in Spanish. She created a worksheet with multiple clocks drawn on a sheet of paper, each with the hands of the clock pointing to a different time. The objective of this exercise was for each student to read the time on the clock, and then learn how to pronounce that time in Spanish. After passing out the worksheets, to her class of honor students, one of the students raised their hand and said, "What is this?"

My wife responded, "It's a sheet full of clocks with different times on them, and I need you to read what time it is and tell me how to pronounce it in Spanish."

The student replied, "We can't read a clock like this!" The student had never been taught to read an analog clock.

For many of us, it's hard to imagine someone not being able to look at the hands on the face of a clock and tell the time. The digital age has made the ability to read an analog clock obsolete. Telling time is vital to how we succeed and function as a people. Without knowing what time it is, how could we ever know when to show up for school, work, church or other events? Without knowing the time, stores, banks, and restaurants wouldn't know when to open or close. Our lives and the society around us would dwell in complete chaos without the ability to know the time.

The same is true of our spiritual lives. If we don't comprehend the times we are living in and the condition of our land in light of God's Word and His imminent return, we will live and function in chaos. Many people in our society and churches are just like the honor students who attended my wife's class; they have never been taught how to know the time spiritually.

Chapter 1 – Knowing the Time

In Paul's epistle to the church at Rome, he instructs them to know the time they are living in and to recognize that we are closer to the second coming of Christ than we have ever been in the history of the world.

And that, knowing the time, that now it is high time to awake out of sleep: for now is our salvation nearer than when we believed. – **Romans 13:11**

It is time for all people to look around and recognize the time! As Paul writes, he is not telling the people at Rome to simply observe and make note of the time. He's not suggesting that they sit around in a small group hidden away in the solitude of their assembly and complain about it over coffee. He is calling them to action. He wants us to look out at this world and understand the severity and wickedness of the times and consider what that means for both believers and unbelievers. We're to let it motivate us to serve God with more fervency and a greater zeal that we ever have before.

Too many of God's people view their local church as a spiritual bunker to hold up in when it should be seen as a spiritual military base to launch out from. We need to lift our eyes and step out from the echo chambers of our own circles and affiliations and see the world through the eyes of Christ. We need to allow the Spirit of God to lead us freshly and freely to do the will of God.

I can assure you, if the problems we face in this world could be resolved by a denomination, association, leadership conference, church board, or any other type of committee, it would have been done by now. Better politicians and bureaucrats are not the solution to our problems. The light we need will not be found in a board meeting but in a prayer meeting of those who long for a move of God and an awakening of souls. We must see the time and know the time we live in if we're going to awaken.

The Culture Is in Crisis

Knowing the times we live in means we view our society with both open eyes and with spiritual eyes. We must learn to see the world as God sees it and interpret it through the lens of His inerrant and infallible Word. Scripture tells us plainly that we are living in the last times.

Chapter 1 – Knowing the Time

Who verily was foreordained before the foundation of the world, but was manifest in these last times for you. – **1 Peter 1:20**

Peter refers to the time of Christ's earthly ministry as the *"last times,"* and that was over two-thousand years ago. How much further are we into the last times? There is no doubt that these are the last times, and the behavior of our culture is evident of that. Sin is not only on the rise, but it is being legalized. Defining the institution of marriage as God defines it—as being between a man and a woman—is seen as discrimination. Designating a person's gender based on their biological genitals is viewed as robbing them of their true identity. People share their beds and their bodies with anyone and everyone, with no thought of saving themselves for their future spouse. States continue to legalize the use of drugs. Politicians deny the rights of an unborn child in its mother's womb, while fighting for the rights of prisoners and pedophiles. Things that people once would have been ashamed of doing in a dark alley are now done boastfully in the daylight, all while posting their evil deeds on social media for millions to see.

Satan's continual attack of ungodliness crashes onto the hearts and minds of our culture like waves on the sea, and it is eroding the biblical foundation upon which this nation was founded. Individuals and institutions who once stood as a beacon for truth and right have cowered under the pressure of the sinful mob. They have turned from that which was right in the sight of God to that which is profitable and politically acceptable for progress. Those who used to kindly say that church and Christianity is not for them now boldly and publicly protest, calling for the banning of Christian principles and values.

The majority of our colleges and universities have been overcome with godless and wicked ideologies. College has become a place we send our teens to spend four years of sinful immorality and secular indoctrination, all the while calling it the best years of their lives. Our children are growing up in an anti-Christ culture whose main focus is the social and legal approval ungodliness. It's time to stop silently accepting unrighteousness and calling it tolerance. Dr. Vance Havner once said, "God judges what we

Chapter 1 – Knowing the Time

tolerate as well as what we practice. Too often we put up with things we ought to put out."

When Paul wrote to his apprentice Timothy, in the second epistle that bears his name, he plainly described the behavior that would abound in the last days.

*This know also, that in the last days perilous times shall come. For men shall be lovers of their own selves, covetous, boasters, proud, blasphemers, disobedient to parents, unthankful, unholy, Without natural affection, trucebreakers, false accusers, incontinent, fierce, despisers of those that are good, Traitors, heady, highminded, lovers of pleasures more than lovers of God; Having a form of godliness, but denying the power thereof: from such turn away. – **2 Timothy 3:1-5***

The list Paul gives Timothy reads like it was written yesterday. Every description Paul gives in these verses is prevalent in our culture. As we read these verses, there is a great danger that can hinder us from ever awakening from sleep. There are many who read this list or hear it expounded upon in a sermon and choose to deny its existence in our culture. They seem to believe that refusing to acknowledge the wickedness around them will somehow cause it to cease to exist.

It's time we stop looking at our culture through rose-colored glasses and see it as it really is. We cannot afford to stick our heads in the sand and pretend it isn't happening. We can no longer listen to the world's justification of sin and change our convictions based on scientific studies performed by the unholy to justify the unrighteous. All it takes for many people to accept wickedness is for a major university to publish the results of a study. If a "study" says a sin is "okay," then it must be okay.

This absurdity reminds me of the State Farm Insurance commercial with a beautiful girl heading out for a date with a hideous, unattractive, and overweight man she met on the internet. On his internet profile, the man claimed to be a French model. When her friend sees this ugly man next to this beautiful girl, he gives her a questionable look. She naively responds by saying, "He's a French model. You know they can't put anything on the internet that's not true." The point of the commercial is that you can't

Chapter 1 – Knowing the Time

believe everything you read or hear reported. Likewise, we don't need to believe everything self-proclaimed "experts" tell us. We must stop drinking the world's cool-aid and heed the advice of 1 John 4:1-5 and try the spirits to see whether or not they are of God.

Let me pause and say that it is not my intention to sit in judgement of those without Christ, but rather to point out the reality of the times we are living in. I have no doubt that many of the people I referred to are convinced they are fighting for what is right, but it is only right in their own eyes. Our culture is headed down a pathway that leads to the judgement of God. Until we view the world as it really is, we live with a false sense of time, and a false sense of time will result in tragedy.

Imagine for a moment that you had an important meeting in the afternoon. All morning long, you check your watch to make sure you will be on time for your meeting. What if you failed to realize that your watch battery was dying and that it was causing your watch to lose more and more minutes each hour? You keep looking at your watch and planning according to the time it reads. If the time is wrong, then your planning is wrong, and you're apt to miss your big meeting. The same is true spiritually. If we choose to look at this world in the light of distorted truth, then we're not going to live and serve Christ with the fervency that the time calls for. It will cause us to live with a false sense of peace and serenity that will end abruptly and shamefully when Christ returns.

It's time for God's people to remove the lenses of political correctness that distorts our vision and see the world through the eyes of the truth. If the Word of God is true, and it is, then neither God nor his Word ever changes.

*For I am the LORD, I change not; therefore ye sons of Jacob are not consumed. – **Malachi 3:6***

*Jesus Christ the same yesterday, and to day, and for ever. – **Hebrews 13:8***

*For ever, O Lord, thy word is settled in heaven. – **Psalm 119:89***

If God never changes, then His perspective never changes. What was right in the beginning was, is, and always will be right, and what was sin in the beginning was, is, and will always be sinful. God does not change His perspective on

Chapter 1 – Knowing the Time

righteousness based on the pole of popular opinion.

We live in a culture that worships the misconception that if everyone "feels" something is right, then that makes it right, but that is not true. Unrighteous actions are not made righteous by the sincerity of our feelings. Our feelings and opinions do not solidify our actions or behavior as being right. I can feel strongly that two plus two equal five, but the truth that it actually equals four will never change. Jesus Christ is truth, and we must see the world in light of His truth if we're to understand our culture and the time in which we live.

How do you view the culture we live in? Have you allowed the continual cry of Satan and the world's system to subtly convince you that it's not as bad as God declares it to be? Have you placed more confidence in the wisdom of man than in the knowledge of God? If so, does that belief not make God a liar?

Seeing the culture as it really is will not be easy or enjoyable. All of us have family or friends that have yielded to sinful habits, wicked choices, and carnal lifestyles. Seeing them and the world as God sees it doesn't make you a bigot or a judgmental person. Is a doctor judgmental when he tells a patient they have cancer? They may not want to hear it, but that doesn't change the truth. Honesty does not make you judgmental. Rather, it allows you to see the need for God's people to become more serious about their service than ever before. It will motivate you to be watching, waiting, and working when Christ comes again. We must see our culture as God sees it and declares it to be in His Word!

The Church Is Complacent

Seeing the culture as God sees it can be challenging, but acknowledging the condition of our local churches is even more difficult for some. If we have any chance at waking from the complacent sleep that plagues the majority of Christians, we must be honest about our churches. When Paul said in Romans 13:11, *"Knowing the time, that now it is high time to awake out of sleep,"* he was writing to the local church in Rome. It's not enough that we see the issues of the society around us; we must also take a long honest look at the issues surrounding our own local assemblies.

Churches are in big trouble. Long gone are the days of seeing new visitors and faces entering our churches because of peer pressure within our culture. There was a time in this country when those who didn't attend church on Sunday morning felt a general since of wrongdoing and shame. You didn't see people out mowing the grass on Sunday morning enjoying a cold one before noon. There was a time in our nation when businesses and restaurants didn't open on Sundays, and the ones that did, didn't open until after noon. Of course, the need for greater profits brought that to an end, and now you're lucky if stores close down on Christmas day.

The struggle of churches is real, and many are closing their doors. If you're reading this book and you faithfully attend a church, you know I'm right. Serious church leaders and members are in borderline panic mode about the future of their churches. If you're not concerned about the condition of churches in this nation, you should be! That's one of the major motivations to write this book. God's people are asleep, and it's time to wake up!

Churches are in trouble, especially smaller congregations. Churches with an average attendance of two hundred and fifty and under make up the majority of churches in this country. Here in the Southeast, where churches split and splinter over the brand of coffee we serve at a fellowship, the average size is usually much less than two-fifty. The point is, we have more people leaving our churches than joining them. Statisticians claim that seven out of ten churches have plateaued or are declining in America. Many of the established churches in our neighborhoods and communities have an aging congregation. In some cases, these older saints are the only thing keeping their church going, but are rapidly becoming limited by their age and physical ability.

Once thriving churches are now barely hanging on, trying to figure out how to keep the lights on. Some don't even meet in the sanctuary anymore to keep from heating and cooling their auditorium. Smaller churches in this country are in danger, and if you are part of one of those churches, it's high time for you to wake up and recognize the time!

Despite the sadness that many smaller churches are experiencing, there are some churches being planted around the country. Many young seminary graduates would rather start a new church than serve in an existing church. In a new church, they can set it up the way they want it to be rather than fight the way-it-has-always-been-done mentality every time

Chapter 1 – Knowing the Time

they want to move the church in a different direction.

Another drawing card for church plants is the popular belief that a church will reach more people in its first ten years of existence than all the other years after that combined. I don't think planting new churches is a bad thing, if they are truly birthed of God. However, planting churches can also be problematic if it's not done the right way. Sometimes, these new church plants, especially if affiliated with a mega ministry, poach talented people from the smaller struggling churches, leaving them in even greater desperation. In such cases, the new church plant can become a source of hostility and opposition to the churches around it. No, it shouldn't be that way, but it often is, and in such cases, it further damages the cause of Christ and validates Satan's commentary to unbelievers that Christians cannot get along.

In the face of the dwindling statistics and the worship wars in small church land, there are some churches that appear to be thriving. They are growing by leaps and bounds with new ministries, facilities, and enough staff to fill an NFL roster. Their pastors rapidly become local legends and are sought-after speakers in their circles. Yet, when you take a closer look at many mega churches, we must wonder if their members are thriving spiritually.

When you step back and look at it, how have they grown so rapidly while others are dying? There are some churches that absolutely have the hand of God on them. The pastor, associates, and congregation are doing their best to obey God and fulfill the great commission. In turn, God is honoring their labor, and we should rejoice in how God is blessing them.

Yet, there are some in the mega church realm whose growth is obtained from acquiring members who leave smaller churches due to their persistent fussing and fighting. The growth of the church isn't due to a great emphasis on evangelism and outreach, but rather the result of people seeking a place to attend with little to no accountability. People go there so they can hide out, not be asked to serve, not be missed when they sleep in or head to the lake, and above all, they'll never again experience the heartbreak of church trouble.

To be clear, I am not trying to bring an inditement against larger churches. Rather, I am making a simple statement of fact. I've worked in large ministries where we saw this time and time again. The heart-breaking thing about mega ministries is that their pews are literally filled with hundreds of talented people that do little to nothing to further the cause of Christ in that church. They become spectators who rarely, if ever, participate in the work of God. Those same people could be used mightily by God as leaders and kingdom builders by serving in another church. Instead of attending a class or singing in the choir, they could be teaching or leading a choir. The sad reality of the mega ministries is that they have become a spiritual retirement home where many gifted servants have become spectators.

There are those who would argue that mega ministries are aiding other churches, reviving other churches, and even planting new ministries. Once again, there are some mega churches who are genuinely involved in assisting and aiding smaller or struggling ministries. Some do a magnificent job at helping struggling churches and work to plant new churches where they are needed. They do so with a genuine heart and in a manner that follows the pattern set forth in the New Testament which allows struggling ministries to maintain their autonomy.

However, there is a growing issue with mega ministries who promote church makeovers that result in church takeovers. Wouldn't it be great if the pastors in some mega churches would go to some of their workers and petition them to go serve in smaller churches with needs? Imagine a struggling church in need of a music minister, a youth minister, or children's minister who could reach out to a mega ministry for help. The mega ministry could then recommend several people in their church who would willingly come help with no strings attached. That's what the apostle Paul did with the church at Thessalonica and Ephesus when he saw their churches in need.

And sent Timotheus, our brother, and minister of God, and our fellowlabourer in the gospel of Christ, to establish you, and to comfort you concerning your faith.
– 1 Thessalonians 3:2

And Tychicus have I sent to Ephesus. –
Ephesians 4:12

Yet, associational bulletin boards, Christian college job placement programs, and Christian job sites all over the land are filled with part-time ministry openings. It would be great if mega

Chapter 1 – Knowing the Time

ministries would send those workers, but they won't. The majority refuse to send help or workers without strings attached. Many of the larger ministries are only interested in helping if they can take over every aspect of the struggling church. Some go as far as to count those attending the struggling churches they help as part of their own attendance and membership. They'll let you keep your church name (sometimes), but all the decisions, tithes, offerings, and management will be controlled from the mega ministry's campus. The end result is that the struggling church loses its autonomy.

The churches in the New Testament were all linked by the same faith and doctrine of Jesus Christ, but each church was autonomous. Each church functioned as a local body of believers, free to govern themselves as they were led by God. I have a wife and a daughter, and we are all part of one family. We're linked together, but we all have separate bodies. My brain only moves my limbs, not my wife's or daughter's. Thus, each church is to be a local autonomous body. The concept of what I call "Chain Churches" is not in line with the church model set forth in the New Testament. The idea of one church in five locations may sound catchy, but it robs the local assembly of their autonomy. If one church aided in the start of five other churches and now each of those churches functions autonomously, *that* is New Testament. However, this idea of one large church taking over a county or region by having multiple sites all governed by one central hub doesn't line up with scriptural model set forth in the New Testament.

If all of that wasn't concerning enough, the approach of our churches is equally as frustrating. Some churches are hunkered down with enough tradition and ritualistic ceremony to choke a horse, while others treat their worship service like a contemporary experiment. Some ministers and church leaders have all but thrown in the towel and given up, while others are reading every church growth book and blog known to man in an attempt to see their ministry grow.

There is literally no telling what you might find going on in the name of Christ in churches on any given Sunday morning. You may find a dressed and pressed pharisee preaching against everything under the sun, or you might find a long-haired lovechild wearing sandals and talking about how Jesus just wants us to unite together in love. It's no wonder people are

Chapter 1 – Knowing the Time

hesitant to attend church today; they don't know whether to expect the doxology or Def Leppard. Even though God tells us he's not given us a spirit of fear, that's all we see in the church. Small churches are afraid of their doors closing permanently, and large churches fear that if they don't find some new act for their Sunday circus their people will leave.

No matter what kind of church you attend, it's time to stop and ask: is our church what Christ desires it to be? Is our church seeking Christlikeness? Is our preaching, teaching, and ministry in line with the Word of God? Those who are holding on to the way you've always done it need to open your eyes and be realistic. You don't send telegrams over the wire; you don't use an outhouse, and you don't store your meat in a spring house. You've adapted to new ways and ideas in every other aspect of life, and you need to do the same in the church.

On the flip side, those who have a pragmatic view of ministry and believe the end justifies the means need to reevaluate their thinking as well. The goal of the child of God and the goal of the church is to glorify God and spread the gospel of Christ. Making the church look like, sound like, and act like those without Christ simply to try to win new converts doesn't glorify Christ.

Don't get me wrong, I think we need to do everything within our power to win the lost to Christ. As one evangelist put said, "I'd give a bicycle away at a funeral if it would keep someone out of hell." Yet, as the great Presbyterian preacher Ian Paisley once said, "There is something worse than an empty church and that's an offended God." We need to make God's glory our goal, and when we labor in obedience to His Word with an absolute reliance on the Spirit of God, our Lord will give the increase.

The problem with so many professing Christians today is that they are just like those students in my wife's Spanish class. They don't know how to tell the time. We've traded sound preaching and teaching for self-help sermonettes that leave us feeling better about ourselves, but with no clue of the time on God's clock. The majority of our congregations are made up of people who never pray, never study God's Word, don't tithe, and sporadically attend church, but because they listen to k-love and eat Chick-fil-a, they deem themselves faithful followers of Christ.

Chapter 1 – Knowing the Time

If you don't realize the mess our culture and our churches are in, then you're simply not paying attention. We are living in the last times, and it is high time that we see and acknowledge the reality of our time. If you don't first know the time, then you'll never see the need to awaken!

2

Spiritual Sleep

*Wherefore he saith, Awake thou that sleepest, and arise from the dead, and Christ shall give thee light. – **Ephesians 5:14***

I trusted Christ at seven years of age during vacation Bible school, and from that time on, I have faithfully attended church. When I think back to the time when I was growing up, it's amazing the things that stand out in my mind. I wish it were powerful sermons or great services where we saw God move, but sadly the things I remember most are the funny and odd things

Chapter 2 – Spiritual Sleep

---

people did. Peter had it right in 1 Peter 2:9 when he called God's children a *"peculiar people."*

With that being said, one of the things I do remember were those people who always fell asleep during the service. Every church has a few sermon-nappers, and all have their own unique technique. For some, their heads bob up and down like a bird slowly eating seeds. Others lightly begin to snore and usually wake themselves up as the snores get louder. One older gentleman in particular would begin to slide down ever so slightly, each minute a little farther and farther, until he was caught by the end of the pew. However, on a few special occasions, his body began to slide the wrong way until he hit the seat of the pew sound asleep. It was like watching a tree falling in slow motion. I don't know what it is about church that makes prime time sleeping conditions for some, but sadly, as a pastor, I too have the touch of sending some into a peaceful slumber.

In this chapter, I want to talk about "spiritual sleep." I'm not talking about those who fall asleep in our services, but those who are in the kind of sleep Paul refers to in his letters to the churches at Ephesus and Rome. Spiritual sleep is not a theological term, but a term derived from personal study, experience, and observation.

Specifically, I'm talking about the condition where people are seemingly unconscious about spiritual matters. They live in a perpetual state of numbness, and no matter the sermon, lesson, or counsel, they remain unchanged, unexcited, and unmovable in their relationship with God. Some are spiritually asleep because they are dead in their trespasses and sins and need to be quickened by the Spirit of God unto salvation. These are asleep and don't even realize their condition.

However, there is another group of spiritual sleepers that are saved, sanctified, and engaged in some form of serving the Lord. They have the Holy Spirit dwelling within them and are alive unto Christ, but their service to Christ is so routine they function more like a robot than a living person. In the next two chapters, we're going to deal with the spiritual sleep of the lost and the redeemed at length, but first, we need to further address the issue of spiritual sleep.

Time and time again in the pages of Scripture we read of God's command to be spiritually awake and alert:

Chapter 2 – Spiritual Sleep

But sanctify the Lord God in your hearts: and be ready always to give an answer to every man that asketh you a reason of the hope that is in you with meekness and fear. – **1 Peter 3:15**

Watch ye therefore: for ye know not when the master of the house cometh, at even, or at midnight, or at the cockcrowing, or in the morning: Lest coming suddenly he find you sleeping. And what I say unto you I say unto all, Watch. – **Mark 13:35-37**

God warns us not to become distracted by this world and drift off into slumber in our service to Him. Yet, so many people today are like the disciples in the Garden of Gethsemane; they're sleeping instead of watching and praying. Just as they heard Christ's clear instructions, we too have heard them time and time again, but we still see more and more of God's people asleep. Their routine has become a lifeless rut that resembles more of the ceremonial rituals of the Mosaic Law than that of new life in Christ.

A believer who has fallen asleep in their service to Christ is in disobedience to God's will for their life and useless to the body of Christ.

God's mercies are new every morning, and we need him to lead us every moment of every day. Our church services have become so planned out and organized due to the growing demands of media that we're not listening for the Spirit's voice to lead us to God's will. We're bound by the order of service and the program to the point that many of us can lead a worship service with our eyes closed. Even though our sleep may not have been intentional, we still need to climb out of our spiritual rut.

It's not only God's people who are asleep; much of the world's population remains asleep in their sin, having never been awakened by the Spirit unto salvation. Christ's death on the cross paid for the sins of the whole world so that anyone, anywhere, could have eternal life. He not only made a way for all, but He's invited all to call upon His name. He has promised to give us eternal life if we would confess our sins and ask him for salvation. Have you answered God's call unto salvation? Has there been a time in your life when you've confessed your faith in Christ and asked him to be your Savior? Each individual must personally accept God's gift of salvation by asking Him to forgive their sins.

Chapter 2 – Spiritual Sleep

When a person has yet to receive Christ, they are in the spiritual sleep of death.

So, is spiritual sleep a sin? The answer is unequivocally yes. People in our society want to argue and debate what is and what is not sin, but in the book of James, we read a very simple definition of what sin is:

*Therefore to him that knoweth to do good, and doeth it not, to him it is sin. – **James 4:17***

As believers, we know that we are to be active and passionate in our service to Christ, and for us not to do so is sin. Christ clearly states in his Word that He is the way, the truth, and the life and that no person can come to the Father but by Him, and yet people are trying all sorts of other ways to get to Heaven. When an unbeliever refuses to accept Christ, it is a sin. If that individual never accepts Christ, it is a sin that will result in them being separated from God for all of eternity forever tormented in the flames of Hell. So, no matter whether it's a slumbering sinner or a snoozing saint, they are both committing sin by sleeping spiritually.

If being asleep and unconscious to spiritual matters is a sin, how do we end up in that state? For those who don't know Christ, they are born in that state under the curse of sin. The saint of God however drifts off to sleep spiritually, much like a person drifts off to sleep physically. I read an article a while back on sleep from Mark Aramli entitled, "The Five Stages of Sleep: Your Sleep Cycle Explained." I'm not a physician and thus cannot verify the complete accuracy of the study, but as I read the article, it was eye opening how the stages of physical sleep parallel with the stages of spiritual sleep.

Sleep Cycle: Stage One

The first stage of sleep is a transitional phase. It's the time when you're going from complete awareness to complete relaxation and a state of unconsciousness. In this stage of sleep, people are sometimes partially awake but become increasingly drowsy. Often, the muscles within the body will twitch or jerk causing you to wake. This is the stage when your mind begins to drift.

This is the same way saints begin to drift off into spiritual sleep. It's not an instantaneous experience. A person doesn't go from being on fire and full of zeal serving God to being in a spiritual coma all at once.

To echo the lyrics of the Casting Crowns hit song, "It's a slow fade." Spiritual sleep happens gradually, and in many cases, people don't even realize it's happening. It's like that one relative at family gatherings who sits down in the recliner to watch TV, and before you know it, they're snoring. They didn't sit down with the intention of falling asleep, but they're asleep all the same.

Sadly, for many people, the transition to spiritual sleep begins shortly after their profession of faith in Christ. They're zealous for a few weeks or months, but then their minds begin to wander. They begin skipping their daily time of prayer and study in the Word. They begin accepting invitations by friends to events that cause them to miss church. It's only one Sunday, they convince themselves, but before, long their mind begins to drift off into spiritual sleep.

Sleep Cycle: Stage Two

The second stage of sleep is the cycle of sleep we spend over half of our entire nightly sleep in. It is a time when we experience light sleep, but it is the time that helps transition us into the deeper sleep of stages 3 and 4.

Several interesting things happen in the second stage of our sleep. In this stage, our heart rate begins to slow as our body enters a restful state. The core temperature of our bodies also begins to drop during stage two. This is why we often find the need for more blankets. Finally, our brainwaves slow drastically, allowing our mind to be a rest.

The spiritual application should be obvious. As people fall further into spiritual sleep, we see the same exact effects as they experience in physical sleep. Those who are asleep spiritually begin to have a coldness in their heart toward their service. They were once wholeheartedly excited and passionate about everything, but now, the spiritual beat of their heart slows. They volunteer less, they pay attention less in the services, and when they used to show up early and leave late, now they show up late and are the first out the door.

The core of their spiritual temperature goes from being red hot to the lukewarm state of the Laodicean church. Mentally, their mind is focused on other things. They find themselves spending less and less time on their relationship with Christ, the growth of their church, or the growth of the Kingdom. They may still be attending and active, but they are becoming more and more ineffective in their service. Their service has become more about following a mindless routine and just filling a space than it is about giving their best for Christ.

Sleep Cycle: Stage Three and Four

The third and fourth stages of sleep are when we experience deep sleep. This is also the hardest sleep to wake up from. On a side note, this sleep must also produce a hormone that wakes your children and tells them to cry out or come bursting into your room to wake you from sleep. I don't have science to back that up, but I do have experience and I'm sure many of you do to.

In addition to being the deepest sleep we experience, the bodily effects in stage two only increase. Our brain waves slow even more, producing what is known as delta waves. The delta waves cause our blood pressure to drop even further, and it causes our breathing to become slower and more rhythmic. During these stages, the body experiences no muscle movement and is almost completely immobile.

I fear that this is where many seasoned believers are in their spiritual life. They've heard it all, seen it all, tried it all, and even though they're still alive, there is little to any change or movement that occurs. Mentally, they experience the spiritual version of delta waves, and their heart for service becomes even less than it already was. Their mind has grown almost completely absent of faith and relies solely on reason and logic to guide them. Their prayer life is talked about more than it's practiced. The attitude toward the church is that it is what it is and nothing they do will change it.

The rut that they stepped into in stage two has now become a permanent resting place for them. Just like the increased rhythmic breathing of stage three and four, their service becomes a rhythmic routine of mindless religious rituals. They've ceased to develop any further spiritually. There is no movement or change in their attitude, actions, or activities. Like the person experiencing deep sleep, they are almost completely spiritually immobile.

Sleep Cycle: Stage Five

If you've studied sleep at all, you've probably heard the term "REM Sleep." This stands for "Rapid Eye Movement." Stage five is the only stage where this rapid eye movement occurs. In this stage, the brain is bursting with energy and is preparing to wake up. We spend approximately 20% of our total time asleep in this fifth stage of sleep. During this fifth stage, the mind is energizing itself while the body is immobile in preparation of waking. This is the stage in which most of our dreams occur. That is why our dreams are so vivid when we wake, because they happen in the final stage of our sleep.

In the spiritual application of this fifth stage, ministers continue to preach, pray, and petition the people of God in ministry in the hopes that the Spirit of God will stir the hearts of those who have fallen asleep and wake them up! Hopefully, they will once again have dreams of what God could do with their life and that they would begin to make preparations to serve God with a renewed energy and zeal. It's the time when the Spirit of God begins working on the heart of unbelievers to reveal to them their need of salvation.

The reality that people are asleep spiritually is not a new revelation. Paul obviously saw it happening in multiple churches during his ministry. However, like Paul did, it's time to sound the wake-up call and petition both unbelievers and believers alike to wake up and live for Christ. We may never accomplish everything God desires for us in our life, but the least we can do is be awake and actively living for Him when He comes. May God help us to be honest with ourselves and others about the condition of spiritual sleep.

3

Slumbering Sinners

Wherefore he saith, Awake thou that sleepest, and arise from the dead, and Christ shall give thee light. – **Ephesians 5:14**

We've established the fact that the world and our churches are in a mess. Now we begin to unveil the source of that mess. As elementary as it may sound, the issue causing the conditions we currently face is the same issue that has always plagued man: sin. It is a foreign word in many homes and houses of worship today. Sin was man's problem in the beginning, and even though Satan changes his approach and tactics with the times, the culprit for all our issues comes back to our sin nature.

The specific sin we're dealing with in this book is the sin of sleep. Sleep? You're telling me sleeping is a sin? Yes and no. Sleeping and resting each night to gain strength to work in the morning is not the kind of sleep we're talking about. We're talking about the sin of being asleep spiritually.

Spiritual sleep occurs when our spirit falls into an unconscious state. We are still alive, but we function as though we were dead. For example, when a person falls asleep, they are still alive, but they are in a state of unconsciousness. Their heart continues to beat, they continue to breathe, and even move, their limbs and senses are at rest. They're not looking around, listening, tasting, or even affected by the temperature. Ultimately, if their surroundings change enough, they regain consciousness and react to their environment, but as long as they are asleep, they remain in that unconscious state. Both believers and unbelievers can be guilty of the sin of spiritual sleep, and in this chapter, we're going to discuss the sinful sleep of unbelievers or, as I like to call them, "Slumbering Sinners."

Chapter 3 – Slumbering Sinners

The fifth chapter of Paul's letter to the Ephesian's is written to believers. Specifically, he is instructing them on how they are to be followers of God. As he moves through the early portion of this chapter, he reminds those who have come to Christ that there is a difference between the actions and attitude of believers and unbelievers—a truth that desperately needs to be emphasized among Christians today. Nevertheless, when we come to the fourteenth verse, Paul addresses the sinful sleep of unbelievers.

Wherefore he saith, Awake thou that sleepest, and arise from the dead, and Christ shall give thee light. – **Ephesians 5:14**

Paul says that those who don't know Christ are asleep and need to arise from the dead. Even though believers and unbelievers can be guilty of the sin of spiritual sleep, the outcome of the sleep they experience is vastly different. The sleep Paul speaks of in this verse is a sleep of spiritual death. That's why he beckons them to *"arise from the dead."* Those who don't know Christ as their Savior are not only spiritually asleep, but they are spiritually dead! What does it mean to be spiritually dead and how can we be so dogmatic about it?

The Curse on Man

The spiritual death of man stems from the first man God created: Adam. Scripture teaches us that after God created the world, He created something in His own image. He took the dust of the earth and formed a creature with two arms, two legs, two hands, two feet, a head, and a torso and then breathed life into it. At that moment, Adam became a living creature. Unlike a newborn child, Adam was created in maturity. He could talk and communicate with God immediately.

Later on, God created a helpmeet for Adam, and she was called Eve. Adam and Eve were not only both created in maturity, but they were created in a state of innocence. When they were created, they were not sinners, nor did they possess a sin nature. They were neither good or bad or righteous or unrighteous. Prior to the time they encountered the serpent in Genesis 3, their obedience to God was untested. They knew nothing of disobedience or the choice of disobedience.

Chapter 3 – Slumbering Sinners

However, God didn't create man to be a mindless robot. He created him to love and enjoy fellowship with. In order to experience the love God desired from His creation, Adam must be tested. Adam and Eve had to be faced with the choice of either obeying God or disobeying God. God permitted Satan to take upon himself the form a serpent and approach Eve in the Garden. God wanted to see what His creation would choose.

God had given Adam and Eve access to everything you could imagine in the Garden of Eden. They even had access to the Tree of Life:

And out of the ground made the LORD God to grow every tree that is pleasant to the sight, and good for food; the tree of life also in the midst of the garden, and the tree of knowledge of good and evil. –
Genesis 2:9

Access to the tree of life meant they would never have to die. Even from the earliest days of His creation, God offered man eternal life. Despite His abundance of blessings toward Adam and Eve, there was one tree that He commanded them not to eat of: the Tree of the Knowledge of Good and Evil.

> *And the LORD God commanded the man, saying, Of every tree of the garden thou mayest freely eat: But of the tree of the knowledge of good and evil, thou shalt not eat of it: for in the day that thou eatest thereof thou shalt surely die. – **Genesis 2:16-17***

This would become the object from which they were tested. When Satan comes so subtly to Eve in the Garden, he is well aware of God's instructions to Adam and Eve about the Tree of the Knowledge of Good and Evil. As he approaches Eve, he devises a plan to mix truth with error in an attempt to confuse Eve and to cause her to doubt God's love toward her. Satan convinces Eve that God had deceived her about the consequences of eating the forbidden fruit.

> *And the serpent said unto the woman, Ye shall not surely die. – **Genesis 3:4***

He also caused Eve to doubt the integrity of God's intentions by telling Eve that God didn't

Chapter 3 – Slumbering Sinners

---

want them to eat of the tree so that they would not become powerful like gods.

For God doth know that in the day ye eat thereof, then your eyes shall be opened, and ye shall be as gods, knowing good and evil. – **Genesis 3:5**

Once Eve heard that she could "*be as gods,*" her fate was settled. She could not resist the temptation of having such power to rule her own life. Eve went to the tree, examined the fruit, and sank her teeth into that which God had forbidden. She then turned to Adam and petitioned him to partake of the fruit.

And when the woman saw that the tree was good for food, and that it was pleasant to the eyes, and a tree to be desired to make one wise, she took of the fruit thereof, and did eat, and gave also unto her husband with her; and he did eat.
– **Genesis 3:6**

The instant Adam sank his teeth into the forbidden fruit taken from the Tree of Knowledge of Good and Evil, his choice was made. They were no longer innocent. Despite everything that God had given them both, they made the choice to disobey. That one choice would affect the lives of every human being to follow. When God came to Adam and Eve later on in the cool of the day, they hid from Him because they were ashamed and naked. God's reaction to their disobedience was to place a curse upon Adam, Eve, and the Serpent. The greatest curse of all is the curse of man's seed.

*And I will put enmity between thee and the woman, and between thy seed and her seed; it shall bruise thy head, and thou shalt bruise his heel. – **Genesis 3:15***

Adam and Eve would both be cast out of the Garden of Eden, and their seed would forever be cursed with sin. Every person who ever lived is a descendant of Adam and Eve, with the exception Jesus Christ. We are all part of their offspring, and thus, we are all born out of a sin-cursed seed which results in all of us possessing a sin nature. Paul expressed this same point in his letter to the church in Rome:

Wherefore, as by one man sin entered into the world, and death by sin; and so death

> *passed upon all men, for that all have sinned. – **Romans 5:12***

The "one man" Paul is referring to in this passage is Adam. When Adam ate of the forbidden fruit, sin entered the world and so did death. Paul gives us a powerful word picture about the effects of sin when he says that *"death passed upon all men."* Sin brings forth death. One of the greatest evidence that we are all sinners is that we will all die. Sin is not something that just criminals and villains are affected by, but it is something that even the most moral and upright person must deal with. Paul is very clear in his description of who is affected by sin when he said, *"For that all have sinned."* On the authority of Scripture, we can definitively say that we are all sinners.

The Condemnation of Man

Understanding the curse of sin is one thing but realizing the condemnation that it brings is another. Adam and Eve's choice didn't just bring about sin, but it also brought about judgement, separation, and death. Our sin nature separates us from God. Sometimes, people say, "I've always had a relationship with God." That simply cannot be true. There was a time in the life of every believer when they did not have a relationship with God because they were separated by their sin.

Our sin nature not only means separation, but it also means judgement. Our sin nature makes us guilty of being unrighteous, and all unrighteousness must be judged and punished by a holy God. Despite what many people believe, God cannot and will not overlook sin. Sin must be paid for, and because we are sinners, we face the judgement of God.

> *Therefore as by the offence of one judgment came upon all men to condemnation; even so by the righteousness of one the free gift came upon all men unto justification of life. –* ***Romans 5:18***

In the verse above, Paul not only mentions judgement but condemnation. The condemnation speaks of the actual payment for sin. God will ultimately judge all those who do not accept Christ as Savior based upon their own righteousness.

Chapter 3 – Slumbering Sinners

And I saw a great white throne, and him that sat on it, from whose face the earth and the heaven fled away; and there was found no place for them. And I saw the dead, small and great, stand before God; and the books were opened: and another book was opened, which is the book of life: and the dead were judged out of those things which were written in the books, according to their works. And the sea gave up the dead which were in it; and death and hell delivered up the dead which were in them: and they were judged every man according to their works. And death and hell were cast into the lake of fire. This is the second death. – ***Revelation 20:11-14***

John mentions the phrase, "*according to their own works,*" two different times in these verses. If we choose not to accept Christ and His righteousness, then we will be judged according to our own works or deeds of righteousness. Unfortunately, our righteousness can never measure up to the righteousness of God. Trying to be as righteous as God is like trying to add inches to our height. It doesn't matter how hard you work at it or how sincere your intentions may be, it is simply impossible.

When those who reject Christ are judged and their righteousness found inadequate to equal the righteousness of God, they will then face the condemnation of God. They will be cast into the lake of fire where they will forever suffer the torments of Hell. This is the condemnation that Paul speaks of in Romans 5:18. It is not only Paul who spoke of this condemnation; Jesus did as well. Just a few verses after we read the famous words of John 3:16, we read of the condemnation of those who refuse to believe:

He that believeth on him is not condemned: but he that believeth not is condemned already, because he hath not believed in the name of the only begotten Son of God. – **John 3:18**

Jesus says that this condemnation already rests upon the lives of those who have yet to accept Christ. Think of it in terms of a criminal who has been found guilty of a heinous crime and has been sentenced to be put to death. That individual isn't killed in the courtroom but is

Chapter 3 – Slumbering Sinners

rather transferred to death row where he or she awaits the carrying out of the sentence. This person is still alive physically, but in the eyes of the judicial system they are already dead. In years gone by, chants of "dead man walking" would ring out as a prisoner sentenced to death was moved about the prison. Jesus is saying that all men are guilty of sin and have thus been sentenced to death. We are still alive physically, but the condemnation of sin already rests upon our lives. Paul expressed it to the church of Ephesus this way:

And you hath he quickened, who were dead in trespasses and sins. – **Ephesians 2:1**

He says that we "*were dead in trespasses and sins.*" The condemnation of sin is already upon us. Think about that for a moment. There is already a place reserved for you in Hell. God didn't create Hell for man, but everyone who rejects Christ will spend eternity in Hell. Many modern theologians and movements have tried to water down the teaching of Hell and even sought to discredit its existence, but Jesus did not. Jesus not only believed in the reality of Hell, but He taught and warned about it.

> *Wherefore if thy hand or thy foot offend thee, cut them off, and cast them from thee: it is better for thee to enter into life halt or maimed, rather than having two hands or two feet to be cast into everlasting fire. And if thine eye offend thee, pluck it out, and cast it from thee: it is better for thee to enter into life with one eye, rather than having two eyes to be cast into hell fire. – **Matthew 18:8-9***

Jesus said that it would be better not to have a hand or a foot than to have them both and to be cast into the everlasting fires of Hell. Hell is an eternal place of torment and suffering beyond comprehension, and all those who have reached the age of accountability face this condemnation. The nicest old lady and the vilest criminal face the same horrible condemnation if they reject Christ as Savior.

Our world is full of slumbering sinners who are spiritually dead in their sins heading down the pathway to eternal judgment. The good news is that it's not too late for them to accept Jesus

Chapter 3 – Slumbering Sinners

Christ and be delivered from death to life. Jesus knows the awfulness of Hell, and He doesn't want you to go there. He doesn't want you to go there so much that He took your Hell for you on the cross. He died in your place, and with His resurrection from the dead, He paid the penalty for your sins so that you could go free.

Are you a slumbering sinner today? Has there been a specific time in your life when you recognized that you are a sinner and asked Jesus Christ to be your Savior? Eternal life cannot be earned through good deeds, morality, charitable giving, or even church membership. You cannot work your way into heaven, nor can you negotiate your way in once you leave this world. The choice of your eternal destination will be made here on earth. So, I ask you again, has there ever been a specific time when you confessed your belief in Christ's death on the cross, burial, and resurrection? A time when you asked Jesus Christ to forgive your sins and to come into your heart and be your savior? If so, when was it?

You may not remember the exact date, but you must remember the day. Salvation is not something we evolve into; it's a decision we make to trust Christ. There was a specific day you were born into this world, and if you have been saved, there was a specific day when you accepted Christ as Savior. So, when was your day? If you don't have a day, then make today your day! Before you walk away from wherever you're reading this book, why not accept Jesus as your Savior? You say, I don't know how? Consider the words of the apostle Paul:

That if thou shalt confess with thy mouth the Lord Jesus, and shalt believe in thine heart that God hath raised him from the dead, thou shalt be saved. – **Romans 10:9**

Everything you need to know about how to be saved is found in the above verse. Do you believe that Jesus Christ died on the cross and that God raised Him from the dead? If so, confess that belief to the Lord right now in prayer and ask Him to forgive your sins and save you. It is ultimately the belief in your heart and the person of Jesus Christ who saves you, not your prayer, but if you're struggling with what to say consider praying something like this:

"Dear Lord Jesus, I bow before You today, because I am a sinner and I don't want to go to Hell. I believe that You died on the cross, were

Chapter 3 – Slumbering Sinners

buried, and that You rose from the dead. I ask You now to forgive my sins and be my Savior. I accept You today!"

If you prayed a prayer similar to this from your heart to the Lord and were serious about your decision, then on the authority of God's Word, you have been saved and given eternal life. You are no longer a slumber sinner, but a saint of God. The Holy Spirit of God has now come to live in your heart, and He will guide you into all truth and help you live for Christ.

If you've accepted Christ, you need to realize that you now have eternal life. You have been born into the family of God and nothing can ever change the fact that you are a child of God. Now that you've accepted Christ, it's important that you live for him every day. I encourage you to find a Bible-believing church in your area and begin faithfully worshipping the Lord there. I also encourage you to schedule a meeting with the pastor of that church and share with him your decision to accept Christ and let him guide you into following the Lord in believer's baptism.

Our world is filled with slumbering sinners and those of us who know Christ as Savior need to be doing more to reach them. That journey doesn't begin by giving out tracts or inviting others to church, but rather it begins on our knees, asking God to go before us, to lead us, and to put His passion for the lost in our hearts. May God help us to be a faithful witness of the Gospel of Christ.

4

Snoozing Saints

He that gathereth in summer is a wise son: but he that sleepeth in harvest is a son that causeth shame. – **Proverbs 10:5**

When you study the life and ministry of Christ it is remarkable how a holy God could be so compassionate with unholy sinners. The love that he showed to the woman at the well, the woman caught in adultery, and to a multitude of others is almost unfathomable.

How is it that Jesus could treat those who were living in open sin with such love and compassion and at times even seem to overlook their sin? The short answer is that Jesus knew they were sinners. He knew they did not possess the ability to do anything other than commit sin.

We don't get mad at a dog for barking or waging its tail because we recognize that those actions are normal behavior for a dog. Likewise, when Jesus encountered sinners living sinful lives, He understood that committing sin was normal behavior for sinners.

For he knoweth our frame; he remembereth that we are dust. – **Psalms 103:14**

On the contrary, when you study Christ's attitude toward His own disciples, we see a completely different response. Christ's speech and instructions toward His disciples were often sharp and to the point. When they failed to obey and grasp His teachings, He did not show the same gentleness as he did with unbelievers.

And when his disciples were come to the other side, they had forgotten to take bread. Then Jesus said unto them, Take heed and beware of the leaven of the Pharisees and of the Sadducees. And they

> *reasoned among themselves, saying, It is because we have taken no bread. Which when Jesus perceived, he said unto them, O ye of little faith, why reason ye among yourselves, because ye have brought no bread? Do ye not yet understand, neither remember the five loaves of the five thousand, and how many baskets ye took up? Neither the seven loaves of the four thousand, and how many baskets ye took up? How is it that ye do not understand that I spake it not to you concerning bread, that ye should beware of the leaven of the Pharisees and of the Sadducees? –* **Matthew 16:5-11**

Jesus was clearly frustrated with the disciples because they were still focused on earthly things instead of spiritual matters. Christ rebukes them by saying, "*O ye of little faith,*" and marveling at their lack of ability to understand and remember His teachings. We see this again after the resurrection in the upper room.

> *Afterward he appeared unto the eleven as they sat at meat, and upbraided them with their unbelief and hardness of heart,*

*because they believed not them which had seen him after he was risen. – **Mark 16:14***

After three years of sacrifice and devotion, Christ scolded the eleven because of their unbelief and hard heartedness. So, why is it that Christ was so blunt and plain spoken to His disciples? It was because when they chose to follow Him, they were forever changed. They were no longer blinded by their sin nature, and their eyes were opened by their faith in Christ. Their acceptance and access to Christ meant that they were now held to a different standard. Christ expected more from them because of their relationship with Him.

The attitude Christ displayed with these disciples is the same attitude He has toward the children of God today. There is a misconception among many professing Christians today that Jesus is in Heaven smiling ear to ear when we make even the slightest attempt to serve Him. They're convinced that Jesus is overjoyed with their minuscule obedience and more than understanding with their abundance of disobedience.

They act as if Jesus completely empathizes with their busy weekends that prevent them from

Chapter 4 – Snoozing Saints

being faithful to church. In their eyes, Jesus understands their commitment to our child's ball team that causes them to miss Sunday after Sunday. They believe Jesus also understands that they can only spare an occasional few dollar for the Lord's work because they're so strapped for cash paying for their new car, those new golf clubs, their vacation, and their unlimited cell phone plan.

It is this kind of belief that causes those who rarely attend church, never study God's Word, don't tithe, don't pray, and never witness to walk around as though they are spiritual giants of the faith. They can be gone for weeks at a time and stroll in shamelessly with their heads held high. It's truly evidence of the sad state of Christianity in our nation.

In truth, God is never pleased with our disobedience, and He certainly does not wink and grin at our sin. Just as Jesus expected more out of the twelve, He expects more out of those who have trusted him as Savior.

Dear child of God, do not deceive yourself into thinking that somehow God overlooks your unfaithfulness and flat-out disobedience to His basic commands. A child of God is not to forsake the assembling of themselves together, and when you do, for whatever reason, it is sin! You may justify the amount you give to God with the same deceptive spirit of Ananias and Sapphira, but a tenth of your income is the Lord's. If we don't return that to Him, then we are like those in Malachi's day: we're God robbers.

Jesus' heart breaks over slumbering sinners, because He knows that theirs is an inherited sleep, and sadly many will remain in that sinful sleep for eternity. However, Jesus is outraged when He sees the saints of God snoozing when they should be working. Jesus tells us that there is a mighty work to do, but instead of working, many of those who claim to be Christians are sleeping.

Christ says that the fields are white unto harvest, but there is a vast shortage of laborers. Too many of God's people are lazy, lethargic, and lackadaisical in their service to Christ. Christians in America have the attitude that we'll serve God and attend church when we don't have something better to do. Our nation and our churches are filled with snoozing saints.

Sadly, the presence of God's servants falling asleep is nothing new. Paul addressed this issue with the churches at Ephesus, Corinth, and Rome.

Chapter 4 – Snoozing Saints

And that, knowing the time, that now it is high time to awake out of sleep: for now is our salvation nearer than when we believed. – **Romans 3:11**

Awake to righteousness, and sin not; for some have not the knowledge of God: I speak this to your shame. – **1 Corinthians 15:34**

Wherefore he saith, Awake thou that sleepest, and arise from the dead, and Christ shall give thee light. – **Ephesians 5:14**

God's people have always struggle with the issue of sleeping on the job. We're like the disciples outside of Gethsemane, dozing off when we should be watching and praying. The fact that God's people are asleep is evidenced by the spiritual and often physical condition of our churches.

With the mass resources of the digital age in which we live, there has never been a generation with more access to preaching, teaching, and spiritual resources than the current generation. We have thousands of commentaries available at our fingertips to help us understand and comprehend the truth. We should be the most well versed and spiritually rich people to ever live, but instead we are a biblically illiterate generation.

Many Christians who attend church regularly couldn't answer the most basic questions about the Bible. They are unable to defend their faith with Scripture, and the majority of what they do know they gleaned from listening to other pastors or teachers. Our churches are mile wide and an inch deep.

Leaders within the church are all too often uncommitted and concerned about the wrong things. When they're not pushing and promoting their own agendas, their main concerns are the church's finances and facilities. In all the churches I've had the privilege of attending or serving in, I cannot remember one time when someone approached me concerned about the lack of souls being saved or people being baptized.

Church leaders and members are all too often more interested in holding on to past traditions than they are about the growth of the church and reaching their communities with the gospel. Our churches are carnal and full of envy, strife, and division. All of this is evidence of the fact that God's people are asleep.

What does a "Snoozing Saint" look like and what are the characteristics of their behavior? When a person sleeps physically, they enter a state of unconsciousness where the body and mind remain alive, but the nervous system is relatively inactive. The body itself is inactive and motionless and the eyes are closed. When we sleep, we are out of touch with our surroundings. We are not learning, moving or advancing, we're merely existing. These same characteristics can be seen in a snoozing saint.

They are alive unto Christ because of their faith in Christ, but they live each day in a spiritual state of unconsciousness. They are indwelled with the power of the Holy Spirit, but choose to live and function solely in the power of the flesh.

You may be thinking that you're not asleep! After all, you're at church every time the doors are open. That is a wonderful testimony to have, but it hardly exempts you from being asleep. Churches are hotspots for sleeping believers. Many deacons, committee members, teachers, choir members, praise team members, and ushers are asleep.

Most churches today are like a sad ride at the carnival. They're old and rusty, sparsely attended, the ride is rough, there's a lot of squeaking and groaning, and when you get off, you've gone nowhere.

Our churches are dying a slow miserable death because we've enslaved ourselves to church rituals and pageantries. We've got religion but no relationship. We do the same things over and over and over again every year. We never pray about them or seek God's will. Our churches are stuck in ruts of routine. Our approach to serving God mirrors that of the wicked.

The wicked, through the pride of his countenance, will not seek after God: God is not in all his thoughts. – ***Psalm 10:4***

The psalmist says that the way of the wicked is to not seek after God or consider Him in their thoughts. When God's people fail to seek God's will and never consider whether or not what they're doing is in line with Scripture or pleasing to God, then we become just like the wicked.

That wicked approach is one of the reasons it's been so long since many churches have seen a soul saved. We have events just for the sake of having events. We never stop and ask ourselves what we trying to accomplish. We never ask if it's even God's will to host such an event. It's fortunate for our churches that we don't ask those questions because the majority of church leaders don't have an answer.

We never spend time in the prayer closet, seeking God for His will and direction for our church. We're content to keep carrying out our own will for the church and have little interest in what God wants for our church. The bottom line is that we're asleep.

We do what we do out of muscle memory. We're not waking up every day excited about new manna; we're stuck eating the same old crusty bread from yesteryear. Our worship services are so organized and follow a set routine that pastors and worship leaders can hold services with their eyes closed. We're going through the motions, but there is no life! The songs are lifeless, the sermons are boring, and congregation is snoring. Dr. Vance Havner used to say, *"Many of our church services start at 11 o'clock sharp and end at 12 o'clock dull."* One of the greatest reasons for that is our enslavement to a religious routine.

In Scripture, we rarely see God repeat Himself or perform the same action twice. There was only one ark, one sacrifice consumed with fire, one man spared from the lions' den, and one time He walked with the Hebrew children in the fire.

But we, on the other hand, keep trying to figure out a divine pattern to do God's work. We want a 4-step plan to winning people and building an awesome church, but it doesn't work that way. The Christian life is a life of following Christ by faith. It is a life of being led by God to do His specific will for His specific people.

Many pastors and church leaders today are so lazy that they refuse to pray and seek God's will. We don't fast and pray over the church calendar, events, outreaches, or anything. If we do briefly awake from our slumber long enough to see a need in the church, we scurry off to the Christian bookstore to find a program that will solve our problem for us. God forbid that we get alone with God and study ourselves and allow God to reveal His solution to the problem. We act as though we're too busy for that sort of thing. Even though we are on the side of the righteous we function and think like the wicked.

Chapter 4 – Snoozing Saints

The greatest issue facing Christians today is the need to wake up and realize the life they have in Christ. We have all we need living inside of us! The Spirit of God will lead us and empower us to see souls saved, lives changed, and our churches filled with revival fire. We don't need new ideology; we need to go back to our roots and spend more time in the Word and prayer to see God move.

Many believers and churches are asleep and don't even realize it. They cannot understand why they're always so unhappy and unsatisfied. They try to keep changing things in hopes of finding the solution. A new young pastor might do it, even though the previous eight didn't. A new style of music might stir things up. Trading in our ties for t-shirts might make people magically want to attend church. A conference with a big-name speaker or high-ranking member of the denominational association might do the trick. Yet, at the end of the day, they're still miserable and making the rest of the flock miserable as well.

The problem is they're asleep! They're like someone sitting in an easy chair and nodding off while watching a movie. They didn't intend to go to sleep, but they're sawing logs all the same. I sincerely do not think the greater number of snoozing saints in our churches are intentionally sleeping. However, most of them are convinced that they are truly serving God and that their lives are pleasing to God. Sadly, their deception doesn't change the fact that they're asleep.

Falling asleep spiritually is so much easier than you might think. Let's consider Peter for example. Peter was a devoted follower of the Lord Jesus Christ. He left a beloved profession to follow the Messiah. He certainly had his faults, but he was passionate in his service for Christ. In the twenty-sixth chapter of Matthew, Jesus tells His disciples that when he is taken, they will all scatter.

> *Then saith Jesus unto them, All ye shall be offended because of me this night: for it is written, I will smite the shepherd, and the sheep of the flock shall be scattered abroad. But after I am risen again, I will go before you into Galilee. –* **Matthew 26:31-32**

We have no doubt that Peter is present and hears what Jesus says because he rebukes Christ.

> *Peter answered and said unto him, Though all men shall be offended because of thee, yet will I never be offended.* – **Matthew 26:33**

Here is a classic example of Peter esteeming himself too highly. Peter is no different than we are today. We all would like to think that our faith is as mighty as David standing before Goliath or Daniel's when he faced the lion's den, but instead, many of us are like Peter. Christ knew that Peter didn't fully understand what he was saying, and so Christ rebukes him with a prediction about his own denial.

> *Jesus said unto him, Verily I say unto thee, That this night, before the cock crow, thou shalt deny me thrice.* – **Matthew 26:34**

Jesus turns to Peter, in front of the eleven, and says, "Peter, you'll not only deny Me once, but three times before the cock crows." What a stern rebuke! That would have made me feel about an inch tall, and I would like to think that I would have shut my mouth and go hide in a corner somewhere. Peter, on the other hand, decides to double down.

> *Peter said unto him, Though I should die with thee, yet will I not deny thee. Likewise also said all the disciples. –*
> ***Matthew 26:35***

It is important to note that Peter was not the only one who felt this way. Scripture says the other disciples also proclaimed the same confidence in their loyalty to Christ.

So, here we have a man who has faithfully served Christ, someone who had forsaken his nets and answered Jesus' invitation to follow Him. He's been warned about his coming denial, but Peter denies his own impending denial! Is there any doubt that Peter is "spiritually asleep" at the end of verse thirty-five? There might be. I think he is acting in the power of his flesh, but I wouldn't classify him as a snoozing saint here. However, when we begin serving God in our flesh and not in the Spirit, we are heading down the pathway that leads to spiritual sleep.

After a quick nap in the Garden of Gethsemane, and a failed attempt at being a

Chapter 4 – Snoozing Saints

swordsman, we now find Peter following Christ at a distance.

> *And they that had laid hold on Jesus led him away to Caiaphas the high priest, where the scribes and the elders were assembled. But Peter followed him afar off unto the high priest's palace, and went in, and sat with the servants, to see the end. – Matthew 26:57-58*

Peter sits in the high priest's palace and tries to remain unseen while he listens and watches the mock trial of Christ. After witnessing the trial and seeing the uproar of the priests, Peter then makes his way outside of the palace. It's only been a few hours since he was so close to Christ that he could touch Him, but ever since Peter refused to believe what Jesus said, he's been gradually getting farther and farther from His presence.

In Gethsemane, Christ went a little farther to pray. When Christ was taken prisoner, Peter followed afar off. Now, he moves from inside the palace to outside the palace just a little farther away from Christ's presence. This is an example of just how quickly any of us can drift away from being close to God. As Peter sits outside of the palace, we see the true test of his allegiance.

> *Now Peter sat without in the palace: and a damsel came unto him, saying, Thou also wast with Jesus of Galilee. But he denied before them all, saying, I know not what thou sayest. And when he was gone out into the porch, another maid saw him, and said unto them that were there, This fellow was also with Jesus of Nazareth. And again he denied with an oath, I do not know the man. And after a while came unto him they that stood by, and said to Peter, Surely thou also art one of them; for thy speech bewrayeth thee. Then began he to curse and to swear, saying, I know not the man. And immediately the cock crew. And Peter remembered the word of Jesus, which said unto him, Before the cock crow, thou shalt deny me thrice. And he went out, and wept bitterly.*
> – ***Matthew 26:69-75***

Three times, Peter is confronted about being associated with Christ, and all three times, he denies. On the final time, he denies with such

Chapter 4 – Snoozing Saints

passion that he even curses and swears that he doesn't know Christ. How can this be? How could he have just experienced such a passionate dialog with Christ hours before about this very thing and now not even recognize it?

Peter was a faithful follower of Christ. He heard the clear message of Christ. Yet, somewhere between the upper room and the porch of the palace, he fell asleep! He was still physically awake. He still looked like the same old Peter, but he'd become spiritually unconscious. He failed to recognize that he was committing the exact sin that Jesus had warned him of just hours before.

If Peter could walk and talk with Jesus and fall asleep, then how much more are we capable of spiritual sleep? Our churches are filled with men and women just like Peter. They'll shout amen and wave their hands in praise on Sunday and turn around and curse like a sailor on Monday. Now, that doesn't mean that every time we commit sin that we're asleep, but there are times when we sin *because* we're asleep.

When we take all of this into consideration, a snoozing saint is someone who has fallen into a rut in their of service to God. They mindlessly go through the motions of "Christian" activity.

They do what they do out of duty not desire. Their arguments and ideas for the church are always rooted in logic, research, and intellect, but never birthed from God. A good worship service is a service where their favorite songs were sung, the pastor's sermon was interesting but not convicting, and where no one did anything out of the ordinary. If you want to see a snoozing saint, just walk into any church in your town and you'll see a flock of them.

What about you? Have you become a snoozing saint? Have you become a slave to your religious routine? Has your service to Christ become nothing more than a routine of activities and responsibilities? Have you stopped obeying God in the most basic areas of faithfully attending church, studying his Word, praying and tithing? Are you numb to the issue of whether your church is seeing people come to know Christ as Savior? Do you not even notice when your church goes months without seeing a first-time visitor? If so, you are asleep!

Dear friend, Christ has so much more for your life and the life of the church you attend. His mercies are new every morning, and it's time to wake up. The second coming of Christ is closer today than it has ever been, and we need

Chapter 4 – Snoozing Saints

to be fervently laboring to see others come to Christ. The light of Christ in our lives and in our churches needs to shine brighter than ever before. It's no time for the saints of God to be asleep.

5

Wake Up Call

Wherefore he saith, Awake thou that sleepest, and arise from the dead, and Christ shall give thee light." – ***Ephesians 5:14***

After my wife and I got married, we spent our honeymoon at a resort in Jamaica. It was the first time she or I had ever stayed at a resort like this, and it was the first time either of us had taken a vacation to Jamaica.

When we arrived at the resort, we found it breathtaking. The landscaping was perfectly manicured and the ocean was absolutely beautiful. After checking in, we headed to the

Chapter 5 – Wake Up Call

room when we spotted a strange looking animal standing in the courtyard. At first, I wasn't sure what it was, but as we got closer it fanned out its tail, and we recognized it as a peacock.

As it turned out, there were several peacocks that roamed around the resort like pets. It was unusual for us to be around them, but their beauty just added to the magnificence of the resort. That is, until the next morning.

My wife and I were exhausted from the wedding and had hopes of sleeping as long as we wanted to each day of the trip. Yet, as dawn arrived on that first morning, we both awoke to some crazy sound that was coming from several different directions. Low and behold, it was the roosting of the peacocks. Every single day of the trip, we were woken out of sleep by those jokers. We wanted to sleep in, but couldn't due to our morning wake-up call.

Many people in our culture today are happy sleeping. The sinner enjoys the sinful lifestyle, and the saints enjoy the mindless rut and routine of religion. They're just like my wife and I on our honeymoon. They want to sleep as long as they want, but God doesn't want them to stay asleep. He wants them to awake unto salvation and unto service.

How then can they be awoken? The answer is simple: those who are asleep need a divine wake-up call. They need to be shaken from their slumber and awakened to the life that Christ died for them to have.

In our previous chapter, we used Peter as an example of how quickly we can fall into a state of spiritual slumber. Peter clearly heard God's warning and was clearly serving Him. Yet, when the temptation came, he was spiritually unconscious to recognize his own disobedience. How did he wake up? How did he come to realize and remember the words of Christ? It was only when he heard the sound of the cock crowing.

Then began he to curse and to swear, saying, I know not the man. And immediately the cock crew. And Peter remembered the word of Jesus, which said unto him, Before the cock crow, thou shalt deny me thrice. And he went out, and wept bitterly. – **Matthew 26:74-75**

Peter had no sooner denied Christ than he heard the echo of the cock crowing in his ears. At the very moment he heard the cock crow, he awoke out of sleep and remembered the words

Chapter 5 – Wake Up Call

that Christ had said. He remembered his strong opposition to Christ's accusation that he would deny him, and yet here he is guilty. When Peter awoke, he ran away from the palace and wept bitterly. He was ashamed that he'd failed to obey the Master's warning.

When you investigate Peter's wake-up call, we note first that it was divinely orchestrated by God. The Lord knew exactly what Peter would do and when, because his perspective is not bound by time as is ours. He knew that Peter was going to spiritually doze off and that he would need a wake-up call. That rooster crowed at the exact moment Peter denied the Lord for the third time because God prompted him to do so. It was no coincidence it was sent by God. The Lord knew that the loud and disturbing sound of a rooster's crow would get Peter's attention and it did.

Wake-up calls are not supposed to be pleasant; they are supposed to be disruptive. They are supposed to be unmistakable and, in many cases, an unwelcoming sound. Yet, they are necessary to wake us from sleep.

God knew what Peter needed to wake him up, and He knows what each of us needs to wake us up. God can use many different things in our lives to serve as wake-up calls. The most consistent tool He uses is the preaching of His Word.

We'll deal with this more in the next chapter, but every time the man of God stands and preaches the truth, God is using that to either wake you up or keep you awake. Dr. Vance Havner said, *"If ever God's people needed to be awakened and aroused and shocked and alarmed to their holy privilege and solemn duty, it is today. The Holy Spirit was given to the church to be a stimulant not a sedative."* God uses Holy Spirit filled preaching and teaching to energize and to awaken those who are slumbering.

Preaching is a fine tool, but it's not the only tool God uses to wake us up. Circumstances, trials, sickness, and storms of life are often divinely placed in our pathway as a tool to wake us from spiritual sleep. There is nothing that happens in your life that God did not permit.

For by him were all things created, that are in heaven, and that are in earth, visible and invisible, whether they be thrones, or dominions, or principalities, or powers: all things were created by him,

> *and for him: And he is before all things, and by him all things consist. –*
> ***Colossians 1:16-17***

If we are facing a crisis, God has permitted us to face it. We have a tendency to blame all of our ills and woes on the Devil, but sometimes they're sent from God. Sometimes, tragedy is the only thing God's people will respond to. It's sad that it takes hard times and broken hearts before some people will awake from slumber to seek God, but it's true.

When you study the history of the children of Israel, you'll see that they were forever forgetting and fighting against what God had given them to do. They were so stubborn that they slipped into spiritual sleep while marching through the wilderness on their way to the Promised Land.

Moses tried and tried to plead with them to wake up, but in Numbers 21, God eventually had to send fiery serpents to bite and even kill some of the people before they would wake up and obey God again. That may seem like a cruel act, but it was actually an act of compassion.

The things we see going on in our own nation today are horrible and wicked, but they have been permitted by God. The continual attack on the church and biblical teachings should serve as a wake-up call to God's people to get serious about serving Him. Whether it is fiery serpents, family trouble, sickness, or something else, when God disturbs our lives, our churches, or our nation, it is done out of love.

God desires to bless each and every one of His children. He desires all men to repent of their sins and trust Christ in order to be saved. He wants what is best for us, and sometimes, He must hurt us to help us get where we need to be.

Peter was warned about his upcoming denial, but he wouldn't heed the warning and guard his spirit. It wasn't God's fault Peter fell into spiritual slumber and denied Him, but out of love He commanded the rooster to crow so that Peter would wake up and get back to God's plan for his life.

The things God uses to serve as a wake-up call in our lives are all unique to the individual. However, our response to God's wake-up call always falls into one of two categories. Either we reject it or we receive it.

The Rejection of God's Wake-Up Call

Chapter 5 – Wake Up Call

It's hard to imagine why anyone would ever willingly choose to disobey God, but it happens all the time. When we look through the Word of God, we find numerous illustrations of God trying to hinder people from disobeying Him, but instead, they chose to reject His wake-up call.

Let's consider the life of David for a moment. No one would doubt that David was mightily used of God on multiple occasions in his life. God's testimony of David was that he was a *"man after mine own heart, which shall fulfil all my will."* David was a mighty man of God, but as my college professor Dr. Keith Kiser used to say, "The best men in the Bible were simply men at best."

David wasn't a perfect man, and even while he was sitting as God's chosen king of Israel, we find him dozing off spiritually. In 1 Samuel 11, we find king David at home in Jerusalem instead of going forth to battle. One night, while he was walking upon his rooftop, he spotted an enchanting woman bathing herself. David couldn't take his eyes off her, and the longer he looked at her, the greater his desire became to have her. So, David yielded himself to his fleshly desires and commanded a servant to summon the woman.

David was not only preparing to commit adultery, but he was going to enter into an affair that would cost him far more than he could ever imagine. In that moment, God in His love and mercy, sent David a divine wake-up call.

*And David sent and enquired after the woman. And one said, Is not this Bathsheba, the daughter of Eliam, the wife of Uriah the Hittite? – **1 Samuel 11:3***

God used a servant whose name is not even mentioned to plead with the king about the sinful pathway he was preparing to travel. This servant asked king David, "*Is not this Bathsheba, the daughter of Eliam, the wife of Uriah the Hittite?*"

In layman's terms, the servant said, "David are you sure you want to call this woman? She is married to another man, a soldier in your army." God was trying to wake David to see the errors of his ways, but unfortunately, David rejected God's wake-up call. Scripture reveals that David never even responded to the inquiry of his servant. He ignored it completely and simply demanded that Bathsheba be brought unto him.

God's wake-up call often comes in the form of a still, small voice, beckoning us to awake unto righteousness and to depart from sin. We even have God's promise that with every temptation we face, He will make a way for us to escape that temptation. Just like in life, we can doze off so quickly spiritually, and when we do the Devil is waiting to pounce.

The Reception of God's Wake-Up Call

It is possible for us to hear and respond to Christ's attempts to wake us. Just as we have an example of David rejecting His wake-up call, we also have other examples of those who received it and changed course.

Prior to becoming the powerful servant of Christ that we all recognize as the Apostle Paul, he was previously called Saul, a well-educated man who was brought up successfully as a Pharisee. Like all the Pharisees, his devotion and dedication could not be questioned, and in his own mind, he was a notable servant of Jehovah.

What he didn't realize is that he was a slumbering sinner. Despite being a man zealous toward God, Saul was an unbeliever. His entire life was devoted to keeping the law of God, but he didn't recognize or have a relationship with the one whom God sent to fulfill the law.

While on his way to persecute the followers of Christ, Paul was met by the resurrected Christ on the road to Damascus. All those around Saul fell down, and Jesus spoke directly to Saul, asking why Saul was persecuting Him and pushing back against the pricks of the Holy Spirit. This was Saul's wake-up call. Christ confronts him about his life and rejection of Jesus as the Messiah.

When this happened, Saul had a choice to make in his heart; would he reject or receive Jesus? Would he awaken from lifeless religion to eternal life in Christ or would he reject Christ as an evil spirit sent to tempt him to sin? Saul chose to yield his life to Christ and received the truth of God's wake-up call.

God's wake-up call is not limited to individuals. Often, God will allow certain events to take place in the life of a nation in order to wake them from their spiritual slumber. We read of that time and time again with the children of Israel in the Old Testament. Another prominent account of God sending a wake-up call to a nation was when he commanded the prophet Jonah to cry out against Nineveh.

Nineveh was a wicked and godless city, but God, in His mercy, sent His prophet to wake

Chapter 5 – Wake Up Call

them from their sinful sleep. When Jonah finally surrendered and preached to the people, the nation responded in a mighty way.

So the people of Nineveh believed God, and proclaimed a fast, and put on sackcloth, from the greatest of them even to the least of them. For word came unto the king of Nineveh, and he arose from his throne, and he laid his robe from him, and covered him with sackcloth, and sat in ashes. And he caused it to be proclaimed and published through Nineveh by the decree of the king and his nobles, saying, Let neither man nor beast, herd nor flock, taste any thing: let them not feed, nor drink water: But let man and beast be covered with sackcloth, and cry mightily unto God: yea, let them turn every one from his evil way, and from the violence that is in their hands. Who can tell if God will turn and repent, and turn away from his fierce anger, that we perish not? And God saw their works, that they turned from their evil way; and God repented of the evil, that he had said that he would do

> *unto them; and he did it not. – **Jonah 3:5-10***

Oh, that our own nation might receive and respond to wake-up calls God is sending forth. I believe with all my heart that the godless legislation, the immorality, and many other things we see taking place in our land are things that God is using to try to call His people back to Himself. America is in desperate need of an awakening and a revival. We need a revival of Christian homes and biblical values, and it must begin with God's people.

One final illustration we see is in the life of Peter. His story helps us recognize the regret often associated with hearing God's call. Notice his response to in this passage:

> *And Peter remembered the word of Jesus, which said unto him, Before the cock crow, thou shalt deny me thrice. And he went out, and wept bitterly. – **Matthew 26:75***

When Peter heard that rooster crow and his spirit was woken to the words of Christ, his heart was broken. He ran away and not only wept, but

Chapter 5 – Wake Up Call

wept bitterly. Peter did not pass off his disobedience by shrugging his shoulders and saying, "Oh well, nobody's perfect." No, it broke him and cut him to the core of his being that he had failed the Lord.

When a believer or unbeliever hears God's wake-up call, it should break them. It should drive you to your knees in shame and cause you to instantly seek God's forgiveness and repent. The fact that we rarely see the saints of God weeping over their sin or crying at an altar during a church invitation is evidence that people are in a deep sleep and not responding to God's wake-up call.

It is impossible for us to see revival or an awakening of souls without first being broken over our sin. Instead of being broken over the wickedness of our sin, we attempt to rationalize it and justify our disobedience. Christians today are trying to serve God without ever dealing with the sin in their lives. Unbelievers want to be converted by attempting to bypass the cross, avoiding dying to self, and refusing to repent. Sin must be dealt with and spiritual sleep is a sin. When God wakes us up and reveals our sin, we must respond.

How about you? Has God been sending you wake-up call after wake-up call through the circumstances of life or through the messages of your pastor? Have you fallen asleep in your service to Christ? Have you allowed sinful habits, attitudes, and behaviors to rule your daily life? No matter who you are, God loves you and will continue to try to wake you to do His will.

Maybe you've been in church your whole life. Maybe you are a well-respected member of the congregation, a deacon, a trustee or a chair person. Peter was by all accounts the leader of the disciples. He was part of Christ's inner circle, and he fell asleep. No matter where you are in your life, it's time to look around and recognize that it's time to hear God calling us to wake-up to serve the King!

6

Blow the Trumpet

Blow ye the trumpet in Zion, and sound an alarm in my holy mountain: let all the inhabitants of the land tremble: for the day of the Lord cometh, for it is nigh at hand – **Joel 2:1**

Trumpets in the Old Testament were called shofars. They were made of a ram's horn and made a very distinct sound. In the Old Testament, shofars were used for far more than making music. They were used as warnings, calling the people for war, calling the people to gather in assembly, or to signify starting to march. The trumpet was a sound that the people of God were familiar with and one that was vital to their way of life.

In addition to being a useful tool, the trumpet is also symbolic of preaching. Just as the watchman on the wall in the Old Testament would blow the trumpet to warn the people of coming danger, pastors preach God's Word to warn their local congregation of coming dangers and encourage them to make ready for battle. Like the Old Testament trumpet, pastors also preach to gather people together to worship and to move forward as a congregation.

In Joel 2:1, we read, *"Blow ye the trumpet in Zion, and sound an alarm in my holy mountain."* Joel was a prophet to the southern kingdom of Judah. Some believe he was the first of the prophets. A.T. Pierson calls Joel the "pioneer of the prophets." Joel prophesied of the coming judgement of God upon his people. God spoke through him to tell the people to blow the trumpet and get their houses in order.

The message that Joel relayed is the same message we need to be sounding out today! We are closer to the second coming of Christ than we have ever been in the history of the world, and we need to be warning people of the judgment to

Chapter 6 – Blow the Trumpet

come. We must be crying out for people to repent and trust Christ before it is eternally too late.

Sounding the trumpet or proclaiming the truth is not the sole responsibility of pastors, teachers, and evangelists. The great commission was given to all God's children. We all have a responsibility to being telling others about Christ. However, if we're going to see slumbering sinners and snoozing saints awake to follow Christ, it must begin somewhere, and I believe it needs to begin with pastors.

The role of a pastor has changed significantly throughout the years. Today, the average pastor is faced with many challenges within the changing culture and approach to modern ministry. Media, for example, has become an enormous part of the worship services and outreach of the church.

As our culture rapidly changes, pastors are trying to remain relevant without compromising doctrine. Pastors are often pulled on all sides by their flock to sway them to lean one direction or the other. Not only that, but we have also seen the death of "cultural Christianity."

Attending church is no longer seen as necessary to be considered a moral upstanding citizen of the community. Gone are days when people would continue to attend church because they felt peer pressure from their neighbors or co-workers. So, on top of their responsibilities of preaching, teaching, visiting hospitals, counselling, and administration, pastors are also fighting to find workers, reach new visitors, and spark church growth.

In the midst of all these responsibilities, many pastors have sacrificed time alone with God. The end result is a lifeless and fruitless ministry. We settle for sermons that are filled with more stories, poems, jokes than sound exegesis. Our preaching quickly becomes nothing more than a short, entertaining, nonconfrontational lecture we give every Sunday. Pastors are giving sermons, but they're not delivering messages from God! In some cases, I fear it is because the pastor himself remains unconverted.

During the great awakening, George Whitfield was appalled by the condition of pulpits in the American colonies. Whitfield said, *"Many, perhaps most, that preach, I fear, do not experimentally know Christ."*

A man must know God before he can represent God. Once he knows God and experiences God's call, he is not interested in

Chapter 6 – Blow the Trumpet

preaching sermons; he desires to have a message from God. The only way to have a true message from God is to spend time with God. That's what we're missing in many of our pulpits today.

We've put our confidence in seminaries, commentaries, and our sermons are as lively as the cemetery. It's not about where you went to school or how well you can interpret the original languages, it's all about being with Jesus.

> *Now when they saw the boldness of Peter and John, and perceived that they were unlearned and ignorant men, they marvelled; and they took knowledge of them, that they had been with Jesus. –*
> ***Acts 4:13***

It was clear that Peter and John didn't have a great education, but what they did have was something you can't earn in a classroom. They had the fragrance and radiance that only comes from being in the presence of Jesus. If we are ever going to see people awaken from spiritual sleep, we must first see pastors awake from the rut and routine of ministry and get back to spending time alone with the Good Shepherd. Pastor, it's time to wake up!

Wake up in Your Meditation

There is nothing more important than spending time each day in the Word of God and prayer. The Devil, your staff, and even your members will try to pull you away to handle what they deem as important issues, but there is no issue of greater importance than that of you spending time meditating in the Word of God.

This book of the law shall not depart out of thy mouth; but thou shalt meditate therein day and night, that thou mayest observe to do according to all that is written therein: for then thou shalt make thy way prosperous, and then thou shalt have good success. – Joshua 1:8

God told Joshua that the law was never to depart from his mouth. God didn't want Joshua to have a message without His message. We must return to being men of the Word, but we cannot preach the Word with power and unction if we don't spend time in the Word!

I wonder how many times God has desired to counsel us on how to handle issues we're facing in our church, but we failed to give Him the opportunity to speak to us through His Word?

The question is not whether God will speak to us, but if we will listen. It is impossible for us to know God's direction for our churches, our ministries, or our own lives if we don't read His Word.

It's no wonder that our churches and ministries are not prosperous and filled with good success when we fail to walk with God. Pastor, it is time to stop reading blogs, arguing over petty associational issues, and watching mega church pastors on YouTube. It is time to dust off the prayer closet and get alone with God again. It's time to call out to God and seek His will for your church and ministry instead of your own. It's time to stop cleaning and cooking with Martha in the kitchen and go sit by Mary at Jesus' feet!

Wake up in Your Message

Pastor, there are many areas we must wake up in, but one of them is in your message.

The Pastor's Delivery

If there is one thing I hate, it is to hear people criticize their pastor. Pastors are not perfect people, but a true man of God should be honored and respected. What I am about to say is not meant to be critical but helpful.

All preachers and all preaching are different and unique. Some men like to stomp around, wave their arms, shout, sweat, and preach till they can't speak. Others like to stand in one spot, rarely raise their voice, read from a manuscript, and only preach for a specific amount of time. Some are more conversational in their delivery, while others are bound to an outline. God has made us all different, and we must be true to who we are.

John the Baptist was certainly different than the Apostle Paul, but God used them both in a powerful way. The issue is not *how* you preach, but rather *what* you preach. No matter what your style of preaching is, the message should always be saturated in God's Word with Christ as the focal point. No matter what our text, our goal should always be to rightly divide the Word of Truth. The Word of God is powerful, and it is what God has promised would not return unto us void. We need a revival of preaching the Word of God!

Preach the word; be instant in season, out of season; reprove, rebuke, exhort with

> *all longsuffering and doctrine. – **2 Timothy 4:2***

The Pastor's Danger

Preaching every week, and multiple times a week, is far more challenging than any non-preacher can imagine. Along with that challenge comes several dangers and pitfalls that pastors can fall into.

The Danger of Perfection

A danger for some pastors is trying to make everything about their message perfect. They spend countless hours combing through their messages with a fine-tooth comb, trying to make sure everything is eloquent and profound. With many pastors' messages going out on the radio, internet, and television, some become more focused on how those audiences will receive their message than on how their own flock will receive it.

I hate to burst your bubble, dear pastor, but no matter how perfect that message may be put together and delivered on Sunday, the majority of your congregation won't remember the title of it by Tuesday. Don't waste time trying to build perfect sermons.

Right after God called me to preach, I attended a large outdoor meeting with a well-known pastor and evangelist in my region of the world. I was so excited because I'd never heard him. To this day, I can remember how disappointed I was with the content of his messages. He was not and is not to this day a strong expository preacher, but in that meeting, we saw multiple people come to Christ every night.

God taught me a lesson through that experience: it's not as much about the message as is it about the messenger having God's hand upon his life. Don't try to make your message perfect.

The Danger of Praise

I've never met a preacher who didn't like it when someone complimented his message. No matter how much a preacher may try to downplay it, it always feels gratifying to hear that someone liked what you had to say. However, there is a danger that lies with enjoying that gratification too much.

Pastors can begin to prepare and preach to receive that praise. Preachers can fall into the trap of searching for that one spiritual nugget that they are convinced no other preacher has ever found. They can also seek praise by trying to preach harder and harder. The bottom line is that when we're wondering what our congregation is thinking while we're preaching, we're in danger of preaching for praise.

At the end of the day, preaching is nothing more than you relaying God's message to God's people. It's not about you, and it's not about whether they love it or hate it. As pastors, we need to do all we can to train ourselves to tune out the good and bad commentary of our congregation about our preaching.

If you live for their praise, then you'll die by their criticism. The only praise we should seek is that of our Heavenly Father saying, "Well done thou good and faithful servant."

The Danger of Procrastination

I hate to say this, but there are a lot of lazy pastors out there. Anyone whose attended a seminary recognizes those who are going to be lazy pastors. They are more interested in being administrators than servants.

Pastor, don't be lazy. Don't procrastinate in the area of your preaching. I recognize that the grind of ministry can be overwhelming at times, but let some of those other things go before you sacrifice your preparation to preach.

I'm going to say something that will inevitably upset some, but if you are using a book of sermons you bought from the Christian bookstore to preach every week, just STOP! I'm not saying you can't utilize them for study or assistance, but if you're using them to save time and simply repeating what someone else preached, you're doing your congregation a disservice.

If I was attending or serving in a church where the pastor was doing that, I'd either leave or as lovingly as I could, ask him to speak to us from his heart on things that God has spoken to him about.

You may not feel that you have any other choice. Perhaps you feel that your responsibilities as the pastor are taking all your time. If so, then it's time to go to your deacons, take a look at Acts 6, and charge them to start serving tables and tending to the widows. You may have to take a hard stand on it, but you cannot forsake the ministry of the Word and prayer and be a pastor pleasing to the Lord. Don't procrastinate on your message.

Chapter 6 – Blow the Trumpet

The Pastor's Doctrine

For if the trumpet give an uncertain sound, who shall prepare himself to the battle? – 1 Corinthians 14:8

We cannot see people awaken from spiritual sleep if we're only willing to play certain notes. Low attendance and the growing unfaithfulness of members can paralyze a pastor. Perhaps you've found yourself in a place where you are afraid to preach on sin or call out the need for repentance for fear of offending the remaining faithful few. However, we must not let that deter us from preaching the Word line upon line and precept upon precept. A pastor should never preach at someone or to intentionally offend someone, but we cannot be afraid of speaking the truth in love.

If our churches have any chance of seeing the snoozing saints awaken to serve God, we must sound the trumpet! If we want to see the lost come to Christ in our community, we must sound the trumpet! Sinners will never get saved without the gospel, and saints will never repent without being challenged and convicted by the truth. The gospel is still powerful, and God will still save.

The question then lies with you, pastor. Will you sound the trumpet so they can hear the warning of God? Will you be faithful to preach and teach sound doctrine? Many pastors have abandoned doctrinal preaching and replaced it with messages on life application. We certainly need to help people make the application of Scripture to their own lives, but we cannot forsake doctrine.

We are not called to be spiritual self-help therapists. Doctrine is like the skeletal structure in our bodies, it's what holds everything together. As our world continues to grow more hostile to the faith, we must be teaching people sound doctrine. It's not enough to tell people what to believe, we must be showing them why they should believe and how to defend their faith.

Bible doctrine should be interwoven within every message we preach.

The Pastor's Duty

How then shall they call on him in whom they have not believed? and how shall they believe in him of whom they have not

Chapter 6 – Blow the Trumpet

heard? and how shall they hear without a preacher? – Romans 10:14

Pastoring can be a horrible, unthankful, and unfulfilling job. The hours are long, and the appreciation is short. The critics are relentless, and the supporters are silent. However, there has never been a greater need for God's men to stand up with God's message than right now.

I know you may be tired, weary, and ready to throw in the towel, but I pray that God will throw the towel right back at you because we need you!

In Judges 8, Gideon and his three-hundred were tired from the battle, but there was still more work to be done. Scripture describes them by saying they were *"faint yet pursuing."*

And Gideon came to Jordan, and passed over, he, and the three hundred men that were with him, faint, yet pursuing them. – Judges 8:4

I know many of you are tired of the fight. You're tired of the frustration and trying to beg and plead with the unfaithful to be faithful and to see the uncommitted commit. I honestly understand, but there is still ground to pursue. There are still souls to be saved. There is still a generation to reach.

Maybe you need to do as Dr. Vance Havner said, "Go apart so you don't come apart." Maybe it's time to take a week off and ask God to restore your heart, passion, and vision for your church. God will strengthen you and help you, but you cannot stop blowing the trumpet. We need you to wake up and preach the Word!

Wake Up in Your Methods

We've dealt with our need to spend time alone with God and the need to get back to preaching the Book, but let's talk for a moment about your approach to ministry.

Churches today have become overloaded with different methods of ministry. Church members look like bees swarming around a hive going in all different directions. There's no question we're busy, but are we accomplishing anything? Greater still, are we accomplishing God's will?

There are thousands of things your church can be involved in, and the majority of them are not bad things, but are they God's thing? Most churches today mistake motion for progress and activity for spirituality. They think because they're constantly going and going that God must be pleased. God is more pleased with our obedience than he is our sacrifice.

And Samuel said, Hath the LORD as great delight in burnt offerings and sacrifices, as in obeying the voice of the LORD? Behold, to obey is better than sacrifice, and to hearken than the fat of rams. – **1 Samuel 15:22**

The ministries of our church are only pleasing to God when they are done in obedience to Him. Sadly, most churches and church leaders have never stopped long enough to see if what they're doing is God's will or in line with God's Word. We push our ideas and agenda through as fast as possible, print up some t-shirts, and then ask God to give us His rubber stamp of approval. Ministries should be birthed of God in the heart of his people. They should begin with God putting a burden on the heart of someone and then moving on that person to develop it.

But ministry today is too much monkey-see, monkey-do. The church down the road is having a car wash, so we're going to have a car wash.

The mega church up the street has this ministry, so we're going to start this ministry. We need to stop looking around at what others are doing or what's popular in the Christian catalog and start seeking God for what we should do.

Every church is uniquely designed by God to accomplish His specific will for that ministry and community. We need to stop playing copycat and start seeking God's will.

Dr. Bobby Roberson was a precious man of God. He was the pastor of the Gospel Light Baptist Church in Walkertown, NC, for many years. If you were to talk to anyone about this church in its heyday, you would have heard them talk about their amazing bus ministry. They had dozens of school buses that they took out into the community to pick up children and adults to bring to church. This ministry saw hundreds and hundreds of people come to Christ.

How did Dr. Roberson come up with such a great idea? He would often tell the story of driving to church and seeing children playing on Sunday. God began to burden his heart about the souls of those children. He began to pray and pray, and God finally put it in his heart to get a bus and invite them to church. That was the beginning of that wonderful ministry.

Chapter 6 – Blow the Trumpet

See, God allowed him to see a need and then He led him on how to fulfill that need. They didn't have a bus ministry to boost their attendance. They didn't do it because another church had a successful bus ministry. They had it because it was God's will for the Gospel Light Baptist Church, and He birthed it in the heart of their pastor.

Many other churches have tried to have bus ministries but failed at it. Why? It is because they were trying to imitate a ministry instead of allowing God to create a ministry specific for them.

The same concept we're talking about for ministries is equally true and applicable when it comes to our worship. Some churches and pastors are focused solely on trying to keep up with the latest religious trends and fads. They believe this is the real key to reaching people. The attitude of this ideology seems to believe that if it's different that makes it divine.

I am certainly a believer in utilizing technology as much as possible to share the gospel. I also believe our churches should represent the time we live in. If your church looks and functions exactly like it did in the seventies, it's probably not reaching young families.

Paint, decorations, and technology are not doctrinal issues. Our churches need to utilize modern technology and appear that they belong in this century.

However, the success of a ministry is not going to be determined by the accent lights, whether you preach in a suit or a polo shirt, or whether your praise team sings the best of K-Love. God is looking for a people who will worship Him in spirit and in truth. God is concerned with the condition of your heart. We need to be who God has called us to be.

John the Baptist was the forerunner of Christ, and he certainly wasn't a sophisticated man dressed and pressed, but God used him mightily. We must learn to accept who we are and who we are not.

I am not a pastor who can preach in shorts and a t-shirt. It is my conviction that when I'm preaching God's Word, I'm representing the King of Kings and Lord of Lords, and I want to look my best. That is my heart about it. So, for me to try to change who I am, how I dress, and what I believe is right in an attempt to reach more people would make me a hypocrite.

Chapter 6 – Blow the Trumpet

That doesn't mean that I am not trying to continually improve and become a better pastor and preacher, but I have to be who I am.

As a pastor, you need to be who you are and who God called you to be. You need to have strong convictions about why you are doing what you do and make certain that what you are doing is in accordance with God's Word.

I do not believe we are far from hearing the trumpet sound at the return of the Lord Jesus. Our world continues to move further and further from the truth, and it's time to blow the trumpet loud and long.

Our cities and communities are in desperate need for local churches to be strong and of good courage, fighting against the darkness of this age. We need to be the light of Christ. However, we'll not be strong and we'll not win the lost unless we wake up.

Pastors, teachers, and evangelists, I petition you to wake up and blow the trumpet so that God might wake up His people and those who need to be saved.

7

Waking Up

Awake to righteousness, and sin not; for some have not the knowledge of God: I speak this to your shame. – **1 Corinthians 15:34**

When I was a young boy, I used to love to go fishing with my grandfather. He was an avid crappie fisherman, and every year, he would try to take me fishing at least once or twice. We had some great days together on the lake whether we caught fish or not. I loved everything about going fishing with my grandfather except one thing: waking up so early.

Chapter 7 – Waking Up

My grandfather was part of a generation that believed if you weren't up at or before the sunrise, then you were just lazy. He applied that same philosophy to going fishing. He would get everything laid out, gassed up, and ready to go the night before so we could head out before daylight. We need to be on the water right at daylight, he used to say.

In his defense, there is nothing more beautiful than heading out on the lake and watching the sun come up. Once I got up and out there, I loved it, but I hated waking up to go.

The world is filled with early birds and night owls. The early birds can't figure out why the night owls want to sleep the day away, and the night owls can't figure out what the big deal is about being up before the crack of dawn. Some people wake up easier than others, and others fight waking up with every fiber of their being.

The same thing is true spiritually. There are those who are very sensitive to God's wake-up call and the sound of the trumpet blowing, while others seem almost deaf to it.

As a pastor, there are those who seem to be moved and drawn closer to God with just a gentle nudge or whisper of the Spirit of God. While others wouldn't say, "Amen," if a gale force wind of the Spirit moved in their hearts. Some people are in a deeper sleep than others and some awake more easily than others, but no matter whether it's easy or difficult, people need to wake up!

In our previous chapters, we've dealt with the fact that God sends wake-up calls into our lives. Sometimes, He uses events or circumstances, and other times, He may use the preaching or teaching of His Word.

In Peter's case, He used the crowing of a rooster to serve as His divine alarm clock. No matter what God chooses to try to wake us up, it is important to surrender to the sound. There are those who wake up in anticipation of their alarm and others who choose to hit the snooze button. Even though it may seem like an insignificant choice each morning, what you are really doing is choosing to either surrender or to rebel against the alarm.

If you roll out of bed when the alarm sounds, then you've surrendered to the fact that time for sleep is over and it's time to start the day. If you hit the snooze button, you're rebelling against the alarm and choosing to stay asleep when you need to be awake. It may feel nice to crawl back under the sheets, but you are really robbing

Chapter 7 – Waking Up

yourself of time that you could be making progress with your day.

When God sends a wake-up call into your life, you have the same choice. You will either surrender to the alarm and awake from your spiritual slumber or you'll rebel and return to sleep.

I don't think any serious Christian could argue that God is sounding the alarm through the circumstances of the world. The wide-spread immorality and wickedness we see should cause us to see that we need to wake from sleep and seek the Lord. When I think about those fighting for gender fluidity, full-term abortions, and the rights of pedophiles, I am reminded of one of Vance Havner's quotes about society. Dr. Havner said, "I used to say society was going to the dogs, but I don't say that one anymore out of respect for the k-9 community." Even dogs have more sense than to perform much of the foolishness we see going on in our society.

The sinful society is not the only place God is sounding the alarm. Many pulpits all across the land are filled with pastors crying out like a voice in the wilderness for righteousness and repentance. The real question is how will you respond to the alarm? Will you choose to awake and utilize the time you have left to serve the Lord, or will you reject the alarm and lose the time you have left? Waking up is not always easy, but it is needful.

We know that we need to wake up, but what does that look like? Waking up spiritually looks a lot like us waking up physically. The most noticeable thing about it is change. When you wake up from sleep, you go from being in a state of unconsciousness to consciousness. Your body goes from being lifeless to fully animated. Your posture changes from lying down to sitting up and standing. You go from being stationary to being mobile and moving around. Your awareness of your surroundings changes, and even your wardrobe changes. Waking up from sleep physically is saturated with lots of changes.

The same is true when a person is woken spiritually. There will be significant changes that take place. No matter if a sinner is being awoken from the spiritual sleep of death or a saint being woken out of their religious rut, there will be change. In the gospel record of Luke in the eighth chapter, Jesus casts many devils out of man, and when they were gone the man was changed.

Chapter 7 – Waking Up

> *Then they went out to see what was done; and came to Jesus, and found the man, out of whom the devils were departed, sitting at the feet of Jesus, clothed, and in his right mind: and they were afraid.* – **Luke 8:35**

One of the major issues we see in the world today are lots of people who profess to have been saved, but there is no change. No change in their attitude, attendance, apparel or their appetites. Granted, true spiritual change occurs from the inside out. Spiritual maturity can also take time to be noticed without, but there are some changes that should be noticed immediately.

When a person wakes up from physical sleep, they are not immediately dressed and pressed with their work clothes on, hair styled, and deodorant applied, but they are up and about heading in that direction. Too many Christians today continue to proclaim that they are awake and serving God, but there is no evidence of change. No change in their habits, their activities, their routines or their sensitivity to their surroundings. There is no evidence of spiritual life within. It's almost as if they are trying to animate a corpse. It's up and moving around like someone who is awake, but there remains no feeling, no change, and no life.

The undisputed evidence of someone who has been spiritually awakened by the Lord is change. When a person chooses to wake from spiritual sleep, they are choosing to repent. They are acknowledging that they have been going the wrong way and are choosing to accept Christ's invitation to change directions.

A Slumbering Sinner Waking Up

Earlier in this book, we dealt with the fact that spiritual sleep for some means that they are lost without Christ. Paul described their condition to the church at Ephesus as being *"dead in their trespasses and sins."* Every person who has ever breathed outside of the Lord Jesus was born with the curse of sin upon their lives.

For all have sinned, and come short of the glory of God. – **Romans 3:23**

As it is written, There is none righteous, no, not one. – **Romans 3:10**

Chapter 7 – Waking Up

*Wherefore, as by one man sin entered into the world, and death by sin; and so death passed upon all men, for that all have sinned. – **Romans 5:12***

We were all once asleep in our sins. We were spiritually dead, without hope, and headed for a Christ-less eternity. Unfortunately, just like a person who is asleep is unaware of their surroundings, those who are lost without Christ are also unaware of their sinful state.

Despite being born with the curse of sin, we cannot recognize our sinful nature on our own. We must be enlightened to the fact that we are sinners and that because of our sin nature we face certain judgement. In order to enlighten us, God sends us a wake-up call. God, by His Spirit, will use circumstances or other Christians to make us aware of our spiritual condition. In his epistle to the church at Rome, Paul states the importance of preaching for this very purpose:

For whosoever shall call upon the name of the Lord shall be saved. How then shall they call on him in whom they have not believed? and how shall they believe in him of whom they have not heard? and

> *how shall they hear without a preacher?*
> – ***Romans 10:13-14***

Jesus Christ died on the cross for the sins of the entire world. There was not an individual who has lived or who will ever live whose sins Jesus didn't pay for on the cross. Anyone who calls upon the name of the Lord can be saved.

Yet, God calls preachers to proclaim the gospel so people can be made aware of their sin nature and need for salvation. When a preacher proclaims the gospel, the Holy Spirit uses the preacher's words to enlighten sinners of their need to be saved. God uses preaching as a wake-up call to the lost to be saved!

Preaching is not the only tool God uses to alarm sinners of their need to be saved. Paul didn't come to Christ as a result of a spirit-filled message from a man of God. God used the circumstances of Paul's life to bring him to a specific place where God Himself confronted him about his sin. While on his way to persecute Christians in Damascus, God stopped Paul right in his tracks and confronted him about his sin. Consider Paul's testimony about how God woke him from spiritual sleep to be saved:

Chapter 7 – Waking Up

Whereupon as I went to Damascus with authority and commission from the chief priests, At midday, O king, I saw in the way a light from heaven, above the brightness of the sun, shining round about me and them which journeyed with me. And when we were all fallen to the earth, I heard a voice speaking unto me, and saying in the Hebrew tongue, Saul, Saul, why persecutest thou me? it is hard for thee to kick against the pricks. And I said, Who art thou, Lord? And he said, I am Jesus whom thou persecutest. But rise, and stand upon thy feet: for I have appeared unto thee for this purpose, to make thee a minister and a witness both of these things which thou hast seen, and of those things in the which I will appear unto thee; Delivering thee from the people, and from the Gentiles, unto whom now I send thee, To open their eyes, and to turn them from darkness to light, and from the power of Satan unto God, that they may receive forgiveness of sins, and inheritance among them which are sanctified by faith that is in me.

*Whereupon, O king Agrippa, I was not disobedient unto the heavenly vision: But shewed first unto them of Damascus, and at Jerusalem, and throughout all the coasts of Judaea, and then to the Gentiles, that they should repent and turn to God, and do works meet for repentance. – **Acts 26:12-20***

Paul, who was called Saul before God changed his name, was a very religious man. He was zealous toward God and wholly devoted to his service to Jehovah. Saul was a religious leader and a man whom others looked to for advice and guidance. He would have been the equivalent to a denominational leader or well-respected pastor.

But even though he was religious, he lacked a relationship with Christ. He was spiritually asleep and lost in his sin. Jesus Christ met him on his way to Damascus and confronted him about the direction of his life. God sent him a divine wake-up call to be saved. Saul wasn't looking for God when he set out for Damascus, but God was looking for Saul.

Often, we take things that come across our pathway as coincidence, but what you pass off as

Chapter 7 – Waking Up

coincidence could be divine providence. It might be an expression of God's compassion to compel you to wake up from your sin and turn to Christ.

God uses preaching and/or circumstances to get the attention of the lost, but it doesn't stop there. The Spirit of God convicts individuals of their sin and compels them to repent of their sin and trust Christ. Salvation is not simply doing better! It's not drinking less, smoking less, cussing less, gambling less, and trying to be a better person. Salvation is repentance toward God that results in a supernatural change that transforms an individual into a new creature.

We often use the transformation of a caterpillar into a butterfly to illustrate the transformation someone experiences when they are saved. When a caterpillar is transformed into a butterfly, it no longer resembles its life as a caterpillar. It is not simply a prettier more polished caterpillar; it's completely different. The message of salvation has become so watered down in our culture that we have a lot of caterpillars who tape wings on their back and walk around claiming to be butterflies.

You cannot be saved without repenting of your sin, and you cannot repent without changing. The very definition of repentance is a change in direction. Waking up as a sinner means you accept the fact that you are a sinner, you believe Jesus died on the cross, was buried and rose again, and you place your complete trust in Him to be your Savior. At the moment you accept Jesus Christ into your heart, you are quickened by the Holy Spirit. Quickened is an old English word that means to make alive.

And you hath he quickened, who were dead in trespasses and sins. – **Ephesians 2:1**

At the moment of Salvation, the Holy Spirit gives life to your spirit and awakens you unto salvation. Jesus teaches us this same truth. He says that when a person believes on Him, they go from being dead to being alive:

Verily, verily, I say unto you, He that heareth my word, and believeth on him that sent me, hath everlasting life, and shall not come into condemnation; but is passed from death unto life. – **John 5:24**

Is it then possible for something that was dead but is now alive to have the same exact qualities? Absolutely not! Something dead is completely different than something alive, and so is the case with someone who is lost and someone who is saved. Someone who has been born-again is someone who has been transformed by the power of God and quickened by the Spirit. All aspects of their life are different. Their interests, passions, perspectives, politics, and moral compass are all different.

Indeed, an individual who has been awoken by the Spirit of God unto salvation will desire the things of God. They will have a hunger for the Word of God, prayer, holiness, and attending church. They will be increasingly sensitive to living a life that is pleasing to God. They will no longer be able to mindlessly practice sinful behavior. When they do sin, and all saints do, the Holy Spirit of God will chasten their hearts and cry out within that they have sinned and need to seek God's forgiveness. In its simplest form, they will be a changed person.

If an individual professes to been saved, but there is no evidence of change in their life, they have not truly been saved. There is no such thing as a changeless Christianity. As the old country preacher put it, "The devil can't move out and God move in without the furniture being rearranged."

In the same way that a butterfly no longer represents its old life as a caterpillar, neither does a born-again saint's life resemble their old life as a lost sinner. Sadly, many in our culture have Jesus on their lips and labor in His name, but they don't have him in their hearts. They are still spiritually asleep and heading for judgement. Jesus spoke of this crowd in Matthew chapter seven.

> *Wherefore by their fruits ye shall know them. Not every one that saith unto me, Lord, Lord, shall enter into the kingdom of heaven; but he that doeth the will of my Father which is in heaven. Many will say to me in that day, Lord, Lord, have we not prophesied in thy name? and in thy name have cast out devils? and in thy name done many wonderful works? And then will I profess unto them, I never knew you: depart from me, ye that work iniquity. –*
> **Matthew 7:20-23**

A true born-again believer's life will show evidence of change, but the change will take place from within and work its way outward. Far too many people today are trying to change without but never allowing Christ to change them within.

A Snoozing Saint Waking Up

The spiritual sleep of the lost is horrific in that it will result in an eternity of torment in the flames of Hell. Those who have trusted Christ but have drifted off to sleep in their service and devotion to Christ may have a home in Heaven, but they will not be without their own judgment. Lost sinners will face the awful judgement of their sins at the Great White Throne of Judgment. The redeemed, however, will face the judgment of their works for Christ at the Bema or Judgment Seat of Christ. Paul spoke of this in his second epistle to the Corinthians:

For we must all appear before the judgment seat of Christ; that every one may receive the things done in his body, according to that he hath done, whether it be good or bad. – ***2 Corinthians 5:10***

Whether we realize it or not, all of us are going to have to stand before Christ and give an account for what we have done or not done. The Lord is going to hold us accountable. Every sermon, Sunday school lesson, devotion or exposure to truth we've experienced throughout our life we're accountable for. Peter recognized our accountability to God, and he tells us that it would be better for us not to have known than to have known and been disobedient:

> *For if after they have escaped the pollutions of the world through the knowledge of the Lord and Saviour Jesus Christ, they are again entangled therein, and overcome, the latter end is worse with them than the beginning. For it had been better for them not to have known the way of righteousness, than, after they have known it, to turn from the holy commandment delivered unto them. – **2 Peter 2:20-21***

There are many people in our communities who have been saved, baptized, and at one time served the Lord faithfully, but they are no longer serving at all.

Many of these brethren have been hurt in the church. A pastor or church leader acted or spoke in the flesh and deeply wounded them. Some were wounded by an action or event that took

Chapter 7 – Waking Up

place during a church ministry or outreach. Others still tried their best to continue serving, but the constant bickering and complaining within the church became too much for them. All of these have their own story and most of them can tell it with a passion and artistry that even Shakespeare would admire.

They've got their excuses as to why they're asleep, and they've convinced themselves that it's an ironclad argument that will even hold up in front of Christ Himself. They've convinced themselves that God understands why they won't go back to church and that He doesn't blame them and He wouldn't go back either. There is not a pastor alive who has not sat across from a faithful man or woman weeping over their spouse's refusal to serve God alongside them.

Those who sit on the sidelines every week and no longer attend church or serve God are spiritually asleep. Their sleep is not an innocent oversite but rather an intentional objection. Someone who drifts off to sleep by mistake is a lot different than someone who's taking sleeping pills. God is able to awaken those saints who have intentionally gone to sleep, but it is a challenge.

> *A brother offended is harder to be won than a strong city: and their contentions are like the bars of a castle.* – ***Proverbs 18:19***

While there are those intentionally asleep, there are far more who are unintentionally and unaware they are asleep. Sadly, I fear that the majority of all congregations are made up of those fast asleep or dozing off. The great challenge for this crowd is convincing them that they are asleep and need to wake up!

Most Christians today believe that because they are active in their church that they are thriving spiritually. They're like a person who is sleepwalking. A person who is sleepwalking is active physically, but they are still mentally, emotionally, and spiritually unconscious. They are up and moving around, but they're still asleep.

No one could accuse churches today of being inactive. We have more activities and programs than we have time for, yet our churches continue to decline spiritually. How can that be? It's because activity doesn't always represent progress.

Chapter 7 – Waking Up

We're spending way too much time trying to perfect how to plant and water, and we've forgotten that God must give the increase. The Lord is the only one who can add laborers and such as should be saved. In order to make spiritual progress, we must not only be active, but we must be awake. We must stop relying on activities, programs, trainings, camps, and conferences and return to a complete dependence on God and the power of the Holy Spirit.

If a saved person has fallen asleep, what they have really done is silenced and shut out the Holy Spirit from leading and empowering their life. God's people often proclaim the need to live for God but then attempt to do that aside from God's help.

There are many who are faithful to church, singing in the choir, teaching a class, or serving on a committee who are spiritually asleep. They are doing lots of "spiritual" things, but they're doing them in the power of their flesh. Even though the Holy Spirit lives inside of them and wants to guide them and help them, they never consider Him. Every decision they make is based on their intellect, logic, and reasoning. They're relying on their "good flesh" to guide them.

Not all flesh is sinful. Our flesh or sinful nature can be moral, kind, generous, and even pleasant. It can be lots of "good" things, but it cannot be pleasing to God or accomplish His will. Paul felt so strongly about our need to rely on the Spirit of God and not our flesh that he condemned all aspects of his flesh.

> *For I know that in me (that is, in my flesh,) dwelleth no good thing: for to will is present with me; but how to perform that which is good I find not.* – **Romans 7:18**

In this chapter, Paul wrote about the struggle within himself regarding the flesh and the Spirit. The fight Paul described in Romans 7 is a fight that all serious disciples of Christ have. If we're going to be awake and fruitful as Christians, we must live a Spirit-filled life. We must not rely solely on our flesh and intellect to guide our lives.

As pastors and church leaders, our approach to ministry cannot rest primarily in what is practical, popular, trendy, and rational. We must be led by the Spirit of God.

To be clear, I'm not suggesting that God's people should abandon all reason, logic, and

Chapter 7 – Waking Up

rational thought. As my former pastor Dr. Ed Yount once said, "When you got saved, you didn't lose your mind." Two plus two still equals four whether you're led by your flesh or by the Spirit.

We need to be smart and use common sense when making decisions, but we also need to include God on those decisions. A great example of this is seen in Acts 16 when Paul desired to go to preach the Word of God in Asia. Did the people in Asia need to hear the gospel? Was preaching God's Word not the will of God? Did Paul have a desire to go to Asia? The answer to all of those questions is unequivocally yes. Going to Asia to preach the Word was a "good thing," but it wasn't "God's thing" for Paul. It made perfect sense to Paul's flesh and rational mind. Yet, Scripture tells us that the Holy Spirit forbade Paul from going there.

Now when they had gone throughout Phrygia and the region of Galatia, and were forbidden of the Holy Ghost to preach the word in Asia. – **Acts 16:6**

I wonder how often we have been in pursuit of a "good thing" but failed to yield ourselves to the Spirit's leading and forsaken the "best thing"? How often do we pursue things in our lives solely because they make "good sense," but we never even pause to see whether or not it is God's will?

Paul was sensitive to the Holy Spirit, and thus he recognized the Holy Spirit's objection to the direction he was going. This is the result of being spiritually awake. A sleepwalker isn't sensitive or aware of anything. Too many pastors, deacons, trustees, and council and committee members across the land today are asleep and need to wake up to be led by the Holy Spirit.

Waking up spiritually is waking up to the understanding that the Christian life is Christ living in you and through you. So much of what we're doing in our churches is completely driven by our flesh. The ministries we have, sermons we preach, lessons we teach, and so on are all often the products of our flesh and not the fruits of Christ. We make all our decisions with our natural mind and forsake our spiritual mind in Christ.

Even the way that churches search for pastors and staff have become rooted in the flesh. Churches look for pastors the same way a fortune five-hundred company looks for a new CEO. They poll the people to see what they want. They post their job opening on every search engine imaginable until they receive hundreds of résumés. They weed out those who don't meet the church's set forth criteria and then try to find the individual who "best suits their needs." What a sad, sad day when God's people adopt the methodology of the world's system to find a pastor to lead God's people. That type of thinking is completely contradictory to what Paul told the church a Rome when he said, "Be not conformed to this world."

What hope does the church have when it's leaders carnally conform? Thanks be to God that Samuel didn't take that approach when he went to search for the next king of Israel. Who knows if Jesse's house would have even made the cut. Even if by some chance Samuel did get to Jesse's house, there is no way on earth that David would have made the list. Samuel found God's man by following God's lead. David's credentials weren't impressive and he had no experience, but when others saw a shepherd boy, God saw a king!

It's no wonder churches across the land are so messed up. I wonder how many times the résumé of the man God wanted to be their next pastor was tossed out and never considered because he didn't meet their minimum qualifications? How different the future of so many churches would be if their search committees weren't spiritually sleeping while seeking a new pastor?

The point I'm trying to make is that until we allow Christ to live through us, we are asleep spiritually. In order for Christ to live through us, we must get our flesh out of the way. So, how do we get our flesh and natural mind out of the way? We have to kill it!

I don't mean that we physically kill ourselves, but we must render ourselves dead in Christ. We must wake up every day and voluntarily surrender our mind, decisions, passions, direction, and life completely to Christ's control. Jesus taught this very truth to His disciples and He used a seed to illustrate it:

*Verily, verily, I say unto you, Except a corn of wheat fall into the ground and die, it abideth alone: but if it die, it bringeth forth much fruit. – **John 12:24***

Chapter 7 – Waking Up

Jesus says that the corn of wheat must go into the ground and die in order to live and produce fruit. The same is true with every child of God. In order for Christ to live through us, we (meaning our flesh and old nature) must disappear and die that He might live. This principle is reiterated by Christ in the gospel record of Luke:

And he said to them all, If any man will come after me, let him deny himself, and take up his cross daily, and follow me. –
Luke 9:23

Christ tells us that in order for us to be His disciple, we must deny ourselves, take up our cross, and follow Him. We must not only follow these steps but they must be done in succession. We cannot follow Him without first denying ourselves and taking up our cross.

To help illustrate this truth, consider for a moment if we had a winter jacket, and that jacket represented your life. Now let's imagine that you represent your old nature without God and I represent the Holy Spirit and your new nature after you trusted Christ. Can we both wear the jacket at the same time? Both our arms won't fit in the sleeves and it's not big enough to go around both of us. At the end of the day, one of us is going to have to yield to the other as to who will wear the jacket. Either you can wear it or I can wear it, but both of us just won't fit. The same is true in our spiritual life. Either you are going to lead your life and make all the decisions or Christ is going to lead your life and make the decisions.

Know ye not, that to whom ye yield yourselves servants to obey, his servants ye are to whom ye obey; whether of sin unto death, or of obedience unto righteousness? – **Romans 6:16**

Waking up begins with dying to self or reckoning yourself dead and asking Christ to live through you. The Spirit is the life, and when we try to live for Christ without relying on the Spirit, we are dead. Waking up is realizing that we need to rely on the Spirit of God to guide us, help us, and empower us in every aspect of life. As a child, parent, employee, friend, citizen, or church member, we need to be empowered by the Spirit of God. The same power that resurrected Christ from the dead is the same power that resides in

Chapter 7 – Waking Up

all of the redeemed. We need to rest in that resurrection power to wake us and strengthen us to be the followers of Christ that are pleasing to Christ.

Dr. Wilson, you may be thinking, *I hear the alarm and I'm ready to wake up and start obeying, but where do I start? How do I reckon myself dead and have Christ live through me?*

You begin by realizing that it is not a one and done experience. Our old nature is strong and fierce, and just when you think you've killed it for the day, it rises back up within you. Paul expressed it this way to the Church at Corinth: "*I die daily.*"

Paul literally said that he died all day, every day. With that being said, a great place to start is first thing in the morning. When you first wake up, begin by praying something like this:

"Father, I pray that You would crucify my flesh today and help me die to self. I surrender myself to You completely today to lead me and guide me in all I do. Holy Spirit, I ask that You would fill me and live through me today."

You don't have to recite that prayer exactly. Put it in your own words. The power is not in the words you say, but in the intent of your heart. As you face a crisis or difficult decisions throughout the day, you may have to softly pray to yourself and ask God to crucify your flesh again and to control your actions and reactions.

The Christian life is a continual surrendering of your life to Christ. That's the real summation of what we're talking about when we talk about waking up spiritually. We must learn to submit and devote ourselves completely and continually to the will of God for our life.

Snoozing saints need to wake up all around the world! God is using the circumstances in our nation, our churches, and our own lives to serve as a wake-up call. We cannot continue to go down the same dead, dry, and carnal road and expect a spiritual result. We desperately need a culture change in our churches. We need a revolution back to spirit-filled living!

Church leaders need to wake up and humble themselves before God and seek His face about the direction of their life and the life of their church. Christians all across the world need to die to self and ask God to fill them with His Spirit that they might be victorious in the fight. It's time to wake up!

8

Don't Hit the Snooze Button

Slothfulness casteth into a deep sleep; and an idle soul shall suffer hunger. – ***Proverbs 19:15***

Have you ever lived with someone who loved to hit the snooze button on their alarm? I had a roommate once who really struggled waking up in the morning. He would set multiple alarms to try to help him wake up. But every time one of his alarms would go off, he would hit the snooze button and go right back to sleep.

Waking up can be hard to do, because it means we have to leave our warm comfy bed and face the day. We hit the snooze button on our alarms as a way to postpone the transition between sleeping and waking. As we noted in the previous chapter, every time we hit the snooze button, we're actually robbing ourselves of time we could have spent preparing for the day.

The same battle many have every morning with their alarm clock is the same battle many Christians and churches face waking up spiritually. It's not an easy thing to wake up from spiritual sleep. Often, we're jolted awake through a powerful message from a pastor or evangelist, and we have a momentary impulse to rise up and change. Other times, a national tragedy or personal crisis shakes us awake, but too often it is short lived, and we fall back into our old sleepy habits.

Despite the difficulty, it is time for God's people to respond to the alarm and get our lazy rear-ends out of bed! We're losing battle after battle in this world, and the repercussions of our apathy will fall upon our children and grandchildren.

When God decided He'd had enough from the congregation of continual complainers, He told them that their carcasses would fall in the wilderness. What a horrible fate to live out your days wandering around in circles and never receiving the blessings God had for you. However, we often fail to mention one of the worst parts of their disobedience. In Numbers 14:33, God reveals the effect of their sin on the next generation.

> *But as for you, your carcases, they shall fall in this wilderness. And your children shall wander in the wilderness forty years, and bear your whoredoms, until your carcases be wasted in the wilderness.* – **Numbers 14:32-33**

God told them that their children would "*bear your whoredoms.*" When we choose to remain asleep, we're not only hurting ourselves, but our children as well. We must not delay in our response to God's wake-up call. We cannot wait another day, hour or minute to awake from sleep to serve God in spirit and in truth. With that being said, let's seek to understand why hitting the snooze button is such a battle.

Sleeping Is Easier

My dad has often commented that it's easier to stay sick than it is to get better. How true that is! When we get sick, our bodies must fight to attack the virus or disease that lies within us. Our immune system rallies together and begins fighting immediately. It takes effort to get better. It is much easier to just lay around and stay sick than it is to work to get better.

Spiritually speaking, it is much easier to remain asleep than it is to wake up. If we remain asleep, we can keep on keeping on with the status quo. We don't have to change! We don't have try to start studying our Bibles and praying for God's direction, because we're just going to do what is logical and popular. We don't have to worry about trying to die to self and take up the cross if we stay asleep. We can keep right on doing the things we want to do.

Remember, when we sleep, we're numb and virtually unconscious to our surroundings. Sleeping Christians often become numb and deaf to the Spirit's conviction over their sin and disobedience. It's easier to stay asleep because we can keep on skipping church to head to the mountains, the beach, the lake, the ball game, or brunch with friends and feel no remorse. We can keep spending God's tithe money on new golf clubs, new shoes, weekend getaways or new jewelry. We don't even have to change our rude, meanspirited and critical attitude toward others. Staying asleep is easier because it requires no change!

Sleeping Is Encouraged

There is no doubt that staying asleep is more appealing to our flesh and carnal mind than waking up. If that wasn't bad enough, we have a cheerleader that relentlessly encourages us to stay asleep.

We don't talk nearly enough about the Devil in our churches. We've allowed godless professors and liberal philosopher's denial of Satan's existence to cause us to shy away from warning God's people of his attack. Satan is real, and he is a real adversary.

Jesus believed in the Devil and was tempted by him for forty days in the wilderness. Some believe that Satan led Jesus into the wilderness to tempt Him, but in reality, Jesus led the Devil into the wilderness to expose how to defeat *him* instead.

Nevertheless, we face a real attack from Satan. He seeks to surround us every day with temptation and pathways that lead us further from Christ. Satan pulls at our weaknesses and tries to lure us away into sin through lust, envy, jealousy, covetousness, and pride. The Devil wants us to remain saturated in the ecstasy of sinful pleasures so that we remain asleep to the will of God for our lives. We've become a nation consumed with fun, pleasure, recreation, and vacation. We seek after fun and recreation like a wild animal seeks for prey. It seems as though some people spend daylight to dark trying to plan their next getaway. We are a people like those in the days of the prophet Haggai.

Ye have sown much, and bring in little; ye eat, but ye have not enough; ye drink, but ye are not filled with drink; ye clothe you, but there is none warm; and he that earneth wages earneth wages to put it into a bag with holes. – **Haggai 1:6**

The lie that Satan sells people is that at some point you'll reach a state of satisfaction through materialism or recreation. The truth is, the more you buy the more you want, and the more fun you have the more fun you crave. The men and women of America are addicted to worldly lusts and pleasures.

There will always be a bigger, nicer, better or more voluptuous "thing" than the one you currently have. No matter how great the last vacation was, you'll always believe the next one will be even better. No matter how nice the car you drive or how large the home you live in there will always be one better.

We have a society that is debt up to their ears in mortgages and credit card payments. Their marriages are strained and their relationship with their children are distant at best. All because we're consumed with the trying to fulfil the desires of our flesh. The end result is we are a nation that earns wages to put into a bag with holes, and while we try to fill the bag as fast as we can, the Devil sits back and laughs.

Hell and destruction are never full; so the eyes of man are never satisfied. – **Proverbs 27:20**

No matter how desperately we try we can never fully satisfy our flesh. Solomon had all the riches a human could ever imagine, and his conclusion in the book of Ecclesiastes was that it was all empty and vain.

I sought in mine heart to give myself unto wine, yet acquainting mine heart with wisdom; and to lay hold on folly, till I might see what was that good for the sons of men, which they should do under the heaven all the days of their life. I made me great works; I builded me houses; I planted me vineyards: I made me gardens and orchards, and I planted trees in them of all kind of fruits: I made me pools of water, to water therewith the wood that bringeth forth trees: I got me servants and maidens, and had servants born in my house; also I had great possessions of great and small cattle above all that were in Jerusalem before me: I gathered me also silver and gold, and the peculiar treasure of kings and of the provinces: I gat me men singers and women singers, and the delights of the sons of men, as musical instruments, and that of all sorts.

So I was great, and increased more than all that were before me in Jerusalem: also my wisdom remained with me. And whatsoever mine eyes desired I kept not from them, I withheld not my heart from any joy; for my heart rejoiced in all my labour: and this was my portion of all my labour.

Then I looked on all the works that my hands had wrought, and on the labour that I had laboured to do: and, behold, all was vanity and vexation of spirit, and there was no profit under the sun. – ***Ecclesiastes 2:3-11***

Solomon had the dream that so many are pursuing in the world today. He had riches and luxury beyond imagination. There was nothing he desired that he could not obtain. He testifies, *"So I was great, and increased more than all."* No one had more than he did. He was the envy of all his friends and neighbors. He reached the Mt. Everest of wealth and prosperity.

However, notice what he found when he looked around at that lofty peak. He said, *"Then I looked on all the works that my hands had wrought, and on the labour that I had laboured to do: and, behold all was vanity and vexation of spirit."* It didn't bring the happiness he thought it would. It was a bag with holes.

We need to learn the lesson that God is trying to teach us through Solomon and stop chasing the rabbit of fame, fun, and fortune. There is no lasting satisfaction outside of the satisfaction we find in a right relationship with the Lord Jesus Christ, and Satan knows that. He continually flashes the latest and greatest thing in front of our eyes and mind in an attempt to keep us away from God and sleeping spiritually. As long as we are distracted trying to fill our lives with the mammon of this world, we'll never wake up to be what Christ died for us to be.

So, the answer must be to saturate ourselves with religious activity? Wrong! If Satan can't lure us to keep sleeping with the pleasures of this world, then he'll rock us to sleep with the rut of religious activity. Satan doesn't mind you attending church. He doesn't even mind if you want to get heavily involved in serving and ministering in a church. He'll even go so far as to let you do all that you do in the name of God—as long as it's about religion and not a relationship with Christ.

The devil is not fighting religion. He's too smart for that. He is producing a counterfeit Christianity, so much like the

> *real one that good Christians are afraid to speak out against it. We are plainly told in the Scriptures that in the last days men will not endure sound doctrine and will depart from the faith and heap to themselves teachers to tickle their ears. We live in an epidemic of this itch, and popular preachers have developed "ear tickling" into a fine art. – Vance Havner*

Our nation is filled with religious bureaucrats and fat-cats sitting on denominational boards making large salaries while specializing in telling others how to serve while they administrate. Many denominational leaders and seminary professors resemble that of life-long politicians more than that of devoted servants of God. They're consumed with trying to be the guardians and protectors of their denomination or movement instead of laboring for the Kingdom. They spend their days bickering and fighting over trivial things that have no significance in light of eternity. They've become consumed with being "right" and proving that to anyone and everyone. They think fighting with a like-minded follower of Christ is contending for the faith. They have the same spirit that John had in the gospel record of Mark, upset that others *"followeth not us."*

> *And John answered him, saying, Master, we saw one casting out devils in thy name, and he followeth not us: and we forbad him, because he followeth not us.* – **Mark 9:38**

Christ didn't die for a denomination; He died for the church! If many pastors and teachers in this country were as concerned about the lost souls of their community as they were about their social standing in their associations or circles, the world would have more saints. While many ministers are consumed with their own personal advancement, their churches grow more and more Christless.

Churches today have fallen into the same problem the children of Israel did prior to going into captivity. We go through the motions of serving God, but out heart is not it. Church has become more about the service than the Savior. It's more about maintaining the routine and annual events than reaching the lost and developing a closer relationship with Christ.

Chapter 8 – Don't Hit the Snooze Button

So, do you think it bothers the Devil when a person wants to get more religious? Not at all. The truth is the Devil is a lot more active in our churches than most of our members. He loves someone who is zealous over religious activity.

Consider the greatest enemies of Christ's earthly ministry. It wasn't the drunkard, the harlot, or the thief that tried to hinder the ministry of Christ. On the contrary, that crowd usually received him better than the most religious people of the day. His greatest enemies were the Scribes, Pharisees, and Sadducees. They were so devoted to the rituals of serving God that they didn't even recognize God when they met Him face to face. Who do you think was responsible for leading them down the wicked pathway that led to them to crucifying the Son of God? It was the Devil. Jesus even said that plainly:

Jesus said unto them, If God were your Father, ye would love me: for I proceeded forth and came from God; neither came I of myself, but he sent me. Why do ye not understand my speech? even because ye cannot hear my word. Ye are of your father the devil, and the lusts of your father ye will do. He was a murderer from

> *the beginning, and abode not in the truth, because there is no truth in him. When he speaketh a lie, he speaketh of his own: for he is a liar, and the father of it. And because I tell you the truth, ye believe me not.* – ***John 8:42-45***

There was not a group in Jesus' day that were anymore sold out and serious about religion than the Pharisees and Sadducees, but there wasn't a group any farther from Christ than them either. Their service to God became solely about the rituals and not what the rituals and feasts represented. Their religion caused them not to believe the truth and caused them to reject the very God they professed to serve. Religion is what kept them asleep spiritually, and it's what keeps many asleep today.

I've often thought that there is not a sadder group in all of Scripture than these. They devoted and sacrificed so much of their lives to the service of God, but in the end, all their efforts were in vain. The majority of the Pharisees and Sadducees died rejecting that Jesus was the Christ, and in turn they are in Hell at this very moment. What a heartbreaking thing to live your life devoted to serving God only to end up in Hell, separated from God for all eternity.

I fear that so many people who sit in church pews across this country are going to face the same brutal reality. They've been deceived by the Devil into believing that their good works, their morality, charity, and labor in the church is somehow going to give them eternal life. That is not mere speculation on my part, it's exactly what Jesus said would happen.

> *Not every one that saith unto me, Lord, Lord, shall enter into the kingdom of heaven; but he that doeth the will of my Father which is in heaven. Many will say to me in that day, Lord, Lord, have we not prophesied in thy name? and in thy name have cast out devils? and in thy name done many wonderful works? And then will I profess unto them, I never knew you: depart from me, ye that work iniquity. –*
> **Matthew 7:21-23**

Why is it that so many people hit the snooze button when Christ is trying to wake them up? It's because Satan is encouraging them to go back to sleep. Whether it's to return to a sleep that seeks worldly pleasures or a sleep that is steeped in religious tradition, Satan is encouraging people to sleep.

Sleeping Erodes

When people choose to hit the snooze button and refuse to wake up, it has a devastating effect on so many levels. When God, by His Spirit, is drawing someone to Himself and convicting them of their need to be saved and they reject Him, it further erodes our society. The wickedness and abominations that are being promoted by many in our country and around the world are the result of sinners without God. When a person refuses to accept Christ, it adds another soldier to the anti-Christ army that Satan is assembling. The result is an increase in iniquity and godless behavior.

When the wicked are multiplied, transgression increaseth. – **Proverbs 29:16**

A large population of Americans not only support sinful behaviors, such as abortion, same-sex marriage, gender fluidity, and even age fluidity for pedophiles, but seek to legalize such behavior. They want to legalize drugs and rewrite history. They fight for the rights of convicted criminals and condemn the rights of law-abiding Christians.

What is even more disturbing is that some who support these wicked actions profess to be Bible-believing Christians who are active in a local church.

Christians are not sinless people by any means, but a true born-again believer cannot live in habitual sin without the continual convicting of the Holy Spirit within. Furthermore, a true follower of Jesus Christ cannot and will not promote sinful behaviors that God clearly opposes. The fact that we see such radical policies and absurd beliefs being widely accepted in our nation is evidence of the vast number of men and women who are lost in our country. As the number of godless people grows, things will only grow worse and worse, and the righteousness within society will continue to erode away.

Unfortunately, as the culture erodes, so do the convictions of many pastors, teachers, and church leaders. Churches and pastors have already begun changing their positions and message on controversial issues in an attempt to please people and avoid conflict. They overlook and bypass certain Bible passages that may seem offensive to their congregations. They believe the goal of the church is to function in perfect peace.

I'm reminded of a story that Dr. Ian Paisley once shared about a woman confronting him about his church. He said a visitor once approached him and said, "Dr. Paisley, your church is always in a scarp or a fight over truth. In my church, there is perfect peace."

Dr. Paisley responded, "I've been in many a graveyard, and there's perfect peace there too!"

The point is that we need to be contending for the faith and fighting for the truth! Jesus said in the gospel record of Matthew 10, *"Think not that I am come to send peace on earth: I came not to send peace, but a sword."* When pastors stop preaching on sin and fail to call out unrighteousness and unholiness, then their churches begin to erode. The church is to be the pillar and ground of the truth and the truth never changes. It is not the goal of a preacher to please his congregation but rather to be faithful and pleasing to God.

Chapter 8 – Don't Hit the Snooze Button

But as we were allowed of God to be put in trust with the gospel, even so we speak; not as pleasing men, but God, which trieth our hearts. – 1 Thessalonians 2:4

The church is to be calling people out of the darkness, not condoning darkness. When churches and ministers fall into the trap of trying to please the people to keep the crowd, it leads to destruction. The false prophets of Jeremiah's day took the path of pleasing the people and refusing to deal with the sinful issues at hand, and it led the nation into captivity. Jeremiah testified of that from captivity in the book of Lamentations:

Thy prophets have seen vain and foolish things for thee: and they have not discovered thine iniquity, to turn away thy captivity; but have seen for thee false burdens and causes of banishment. – **Lamentations 2:14**

Jeremiah said that those prophets failed to "*discover thine iniquity.*" That means they failed to call out their sin against God. The purpose of calling out their sin would have been to "*turn away thy captivity.*"

Preaching on sin is not pleasant for the preacher or the parishioner, but it is needful. We must recognize we are sick in order to realize our need for healing. Instead of preaching the truth, too many ministers and ministries promote "*false burdens*" for their people. Churches have become centers for humanitarian and social needs instead of being a lighthouse for the spiritual needs of world. We think giving people free stuff equates to missions.

There's nothing wrong with helping those in need, but when the physical help becomes the central theme of your ministry, you've missed the mark of God's work. God's people are to be giving the gospel and telling people about Jesus. When we fail to emphasize gospel evangelism, it is further evidence that God's people have chosen to hit the snooze button and stay asleep. We must heed the warnings of God about promoting evil and ridiculing good.

Woe unto them that call evil good, and good evil; that put darkness for light, and light for darkness; that put bitter for sweet, and sweet for bitter! – **Isaiah 5:20**

Chapter 8 – Don't Hit the Snooze Button

In a perfect world, when a pastor, leader, or politician started calling evil good and good evil, the people would recognize it and stand up against it. Sadly, in our current cultural climate, many do not. They don't say anything, and some even believe that evil is good and good is evil.

One of the reasons for this is the epidemic of biblical illiteracy throughout our nation. The only Bible many church goers know is what their pastor or small group leader tells them. The majority of people attending church aren't even interested in the truth enough to carry a Bible to the service and follow along.

We verify the accuracy of our fantasy sports rosters and our Amazon orders more than we verify the accuracy of what our pastors are preaching. The decision to remain asleep when God's trying to wake us up will slowly eat away at the foundations of everything other generations fought so hard to obtain. It is much like the illustration Solomon gave about the vineyard of the slothful:

I went by the field of the slothful, and by the vineyard of the man void of understanding; And, lo, it was all grown over with thorns, and nettles had covered the face thereof, and the stone wall thereof was broken down. Then I saw, and considered it well: I looked upon it, and received instruction. Yet a little sleep, a little slumber, a little folding of the hands to sleep: So shall thy poverty come as one that travelleth; and thy want as an armed man. – ***Proverbs 24:30-34***

What a vivid picture Solomon painted with those verses. As you read his words, you almost feel like you are walking beside him on a dusty road in the countryside. Solomon says that he saw a deserted field—a field that had such potential for livestock or crops. It was a field that could have served as a means of income and livelihood for a family. It could have been a source of produce and substance for the community. It could have been left as an inheritance for future generations. Instead, the field was all grown over with thorns, nettles, leaves, and brush. The stone wall that would have served as a barrier of protection and identification was broken down.

There wasn't anything wrong with the field; the problem rested with its caretaker. The one who had been given the responsibility to

Chapter 8 – Don't Hit the Snooze Button

maintain it, work it, and utilize it had failed. Instead of working, they chose to lay around and neglect it.

I can imagine that they looked out at the field and thought, we'll work on it tomorrow. Perhaps they thought that next week would be good enough to repair the stones that had fallen from the wall. One day turned into two and two days turned into a week, and before they realized it, years had gone by.

After Solomon passed by this field, he says that he considered it well. There was a valuable lesson to be learned through the slothful owner and his neglect of the field. The lesson is that when we neglect to act, the end results can be devastating. That which once had such potential can sit idly by and waste away.

The point I'm trying to relay here is that to delay is to disobey! We are only given a short time to serve God on this earth, and we need to make the most of the time we've been given. If you've never trusted Christ as Savior, but you know in your heart that God has been dealing with you about being saved, don't delay another minute. If you've fallen asleep with the religious rut and routine of modern Christianity and God is nudging you to awaken to live a Spirit-filled life, don't delay!

We've seen how easy it is for us to remain asleep, and how tempting it can be to just proceed with the status quo, but dear Lord, I'm begging you; don't hit the snooze button. Don't postpone saying yes to God's wake-up call.

Dr. Clarence Sexton used to tell us that when we read the Bible or listen to a sermon, we should always begin by saying, yes to the Lord. No matter what it is you're going to say or ask me to do, Lord, the answer is already yes. If God is dealing with your heart about waking up to live for Him, say yes.

Don't let your life be consumed with trying to keep up with the Joneses. Don't let the spiritual field of your life—that which has so much potential to bear fruit for God—be grown over with thorns and nettles. Don't hit snooze! Wake up, and let God begin living through you today!

9

The Awakened Church

*And I say also unto thee, That thou art Peter, and upon this rock I will build my church; and the gates of hell shall not prevail against it. – **Matthew 16:18***

There are verses and passages of Scripture that hit my amen-hallelujah-praise-God button, and Matthew 16:18 is one of those verses. I obviously wasn't there to hear Christ utter these words to Peter, but when I think about the absolute power and authority from which He spoke of building His church and the guaranteed victory over Hell, it gives me goosebumps.

The truth Christ shares in this verse is something that we need to remember during these dark days. Christ, the church, and His children are and will be victorious over the enemy. No matter how hard man tries, they will never successfully eradicate the work of Christ and biblical Christianity. Satan and his crowd will lose, end of story!

Unfortunately, the average church today is so discouraged, dishearten, and defeated that I fear they don't truly believe it anymore. Many local church pastors and leaders look around and see an aging congregation struggling to find laborers, meet the bills, and failing to reach the next generation. It's time for us to lift our eyes and look unto Jesus. He is still on Heaven's throne and in absolute control. We need to stop thinking about our lives and our churches in light of our abilities and view them in light of God's ability.

Yes, many of our churches are made up of older saints. Many of them are struggling to keep up with the culture and changes to technology throughout society. Many church leaders feel like they're inadequate to compete with the mega church in town that can hire the best and brightest, while all they have is uncommitted

Chapter 9 – The Awakened Church

volunteers. All of that maybe true, and when the Devil reminds you of it in an attempt to discourage you, tell him that he's right!

It's all true, Satan. We don't have the talent, the laborers, the facilities, the media or dozens of other modern-day Christian toys and trinkets. Yet, we have Jesus. We have victory in Jesus, and Satan might stop us, but he won't stop Him! Declare to that old serpent that you're no longer going to settle for the religious rut and routine that leads to dry, dead, lifeless, and powerless services that we've grown accustomed to. Rather, you're going to answer God's wake-up call and challenge others in your local assembly to do the same. Choose to surrender your lives to Christ and allow the Holy Spirit of God to fill you and empower you to do the work God longs to do.

God's not looking for the most talented and winsome people to do His work. He's looking for those who will die to self so that Christ might live through them. He's looking for those who will obey Him and seek to do His will above their own.

Your congregation is made up of a lot of gray hair. So what? Gray hair didn't stop Caleb from claiming the mountain for God nor did it stop Abraham and Sara from conceiving God's promised son Isaac. A ninety-five-year-old person who has surrendered themselves to Christ and is filled with the Spirit is more valuable to God than a talented nineteen-year-old full of pride and ambition serving in the power of the flesh. The power of the church is Christ and His ability to live through the members of the body. When He is permitted to do that, then the results will be amazing.

If a church chooses to heed God's wake-up call and awake from their slumber, what does it look like? What would the characteristics of an awakened church be? The most obvious characteristics of an awake church is when it begins to take upon it the characteristics of the New Testament church. All their values, plans, and purposes align with God's purpose and plan. The age-old quarrels and conflicts among members fade away with forgiveness. Frivolous and flesh-based ministries are quickly replaced with a passion for reaching the lost. The "sacred cows" of tradition are removed and "we've always done it this way" is erased from our vocabulary.

All the things we've been trying to forcibly achieve for years with the power of the flesh will be brought to pass in an instant. An awakened church will look a lot like the first church in Jerusalem. It will be the emblem of Christlikeness. Let's consider some of the characteristics of an awakened church.

The Cross

An awakened church is a church that is well acquainted with the cross of Christ. When the apostles and other disciples assembled themselves together in the upper room, they had the cross on their minds. The work of Christ on the cross was something forever etched in their hearts and minds. The cross for them wasn't a neckless, a lapel pin, or pair of earrings; it was the place of atonement for sin.

They were witnesses of the horrible torture and agony that Christ suffered on the cross. The bloodshed and heartache of watching their beloved friend and Savior gasping for breath as He hung on the tree was always on their minds. The early church was fully aware of the cost that was paid for their salvation.

An individual or church that is awake spiritually will never stray far from the cross and the empty tomb. Though we do not have the same insight as those present on that day, we can still see the cross and His sufferings through the pages of Scripture and the enlightenment of the Holy Spirit. Christ's death on the cross, His burial, and His resurrection are the absolute foundation of our salvation! An awakened church not only meditates on, but frequently and fervently proclaims the cross and its message to the world.

Like so many other unpleasant things in our world's history, there are those who stray away from talking about the cross because it's unpleasant. Shame on any preacher, teacher, or Christian worker who fails to proclaim Christ's work on the cross. Could it be that Christians today do not value their salvation because we as ministers have failed to accurately explain what it cost? Without His sacrifice, there would be no payment for our sins. The awakened church is not ashamed of the cross of Christ, but instead, we should be proudly proclaiming the glorious work of Christ on the cross.

The Filling of the Spirit

An awakened church will not only be acquainted with the cross but also be a people filled with the Spirit of God. Too many of God's people are fearful and unacquainted with the work of the Holy Spirit. So much of that fear and lack of knowledge comes from pastors who fail to emphasize and educate their congregation about the Holy Spirit.

Nevertheless, a church that is alive and awake to serving God will be a church led by the Holy Spirit. In the early church, we see the Holy Spirit fill all those present in the upper room. Those believers were given special gifts by the Spirit for the purpose of rapidly spreading the gospel. For example, the apostles began to speak fluently in other languages, healing the sick, and performing miracles. It is my conviction that these were special gifts given to the apostles for the purpose of initially spreading the gospel of Christ around the world.

These special gifts of the Spirit are not present in believers today. However, the need to be filled with the Spirit is needed as much today as it was then. We have well documented the need to be filled with the Spirit of God to do His work, and a church that has awoken spiritually will be a church where its members are filled, led, and empowered by the Holy Spirit.

Divine Unity

One of the most challenging things in the world is to unify people. No matter whether it is in sports, business, recreation, or church, it is difficult to get everyone to unite together toward one goal. If you've spent more than five minutes in a local church, you know what I'm telling you is true.

Churches and Christians are notorious for not getting along with one another. Isn't that a shame? Isn't it a shame that so many churches throughout our communities are known for their lack of unity? Maybe you attend a church like that. When there is a lack of unity in a church, it is evidence that the church is filled with sleeping saints who are serving solely in the power of their flesh. Sustainable unity in a church is impossible to accomplish in our flesh. My flesh and your flesh will always disagree because it is our nature to always believe we are right.

Every way of a man is right in his own eyes: but the LORD pondereth the hearts.
– ***Proverbs 21:2***

Unity is impossible in our flesh, but it is not impossible with the Spirit. When a person accepts Christ, the Holy Spirit then indwells or resides in that person. So, if you have two believers discussing a situation, then even though they are different people in the flesh, they are still united because both have the same Holy Spirit within. Unity happens when both parties individually surrender themselves to God and seek His will instead of their own. The Holy Spirit in one then bears witness with and agrees with the Holy Spirit in the other person, because it's the same Holy Spirit. A church that is awakened spiritually will have unity. One of the earmarks of the first church was their continual unity.

*These all continued with one accord in prayer and supplication, with the women, and Mary the mother of Jesus, and with his brethren. – **Acts 1:14***

*And when the day of Pentecost was fully come, they were all with one accord in one place. – **Acts 2:1***

And they, continuing daily with one accord in the temple, and breaking bread from house to house, did eat their meat with gladness and singleness of heart. –
Acts 2:46

Time and time again, we read of the early church working and serving in one accord. They were a group of people united around one single purpose and that was to fulfill the work Christ had given them to do. Unity should be commonplace in local churches, but instead, it is highly uncommon. We not only see unity in the early church, but the Apostle Paul emphasized the same thing to the church at Philippi.

*If there be therefore any consolation in Christ, if any comfort of love, if any fellowship of the Spirit, if any bowels and mercies, Fulfil ye my joy, that ye be likeminded, having the same love, being of one accord, of one mind. – **Philippians 2:1-2***

If you serve in a church where strife, conflict, backbiting, and turmoil are normal, then you're serving in a church that is asleep spiritually. An awakened church is not a perfect church that never has disagreements, but when disagreements arise, they choose to seek God together and yield themselves to His will above their own.

A Clear Message

One of the major issues within churches and denominations today is that our message is not clear. The message of salvation is either not being given or it is given in an unclear manner. The purpose of the church and what the church is trying to accomplish is often undefined, unintentional, and lost in the array of activities. This problem begins with and must be addressed at the top with pastors and church leaders. If this issue goes unattended, it leads to devastation and destruction for God's people. Jeremiah speaks of this same problem in his day:

> *Thy prophets have seen vain and foolish things for thee: and they have not discovered thine iniquity, to turn away thy captivity; but have seen for thee false burdens and causes of banishment.* – **Lamentations 2:14**

When pastors are afraid to deliver a clear message about sin and salvation, people develop a false since of security. They believe everything is okay in the world, and they fail to be made aware of the coming judgement of God. When pastors awake from the rut and routine of simply writing out sermons and get back to the place where they settle for nothing less than getting and delivering a message from God, things will change.

The messages from the pulpit and throughout the church will not only be full of life and passion, but there will be a clarity in the message. All the lessons and messages will have a common thread of exalting Christ and drawing people into a closer walk with Him.

We see such clarity in the preaching of Peter, John, and Paul in the book of Acts. Their preaching was unpolished, simple, bold, and effective. The central theme was always Jesus Christ and the need of others to turn from their sins and follow Him.

> *Therefore let all the house of Israel know assuredly, that God hath made that same Jesus, whom ye have crucified, both Lord and Christ. Now when they heard this, they were pricked in their heart, and said unto Peter and to the rest of the apostles, Men and brethren, what shall we do? Then Peter said unto them, Repent, and be baptized every one of you in the name of Jesus Christ for the remission of sins, and*

> *ye shall receive the gift of the Holy Ghost.*
> *– Acts 2:36-38*
>
> *Be it known unto you all, and to all the people of Israel, that by the name of Jesus Christ of Nazareth, whom ye crucified, whom God raised from the dead, even by him doth this man stand here before you whole. This is the stone which was set at nought of you builders, which is become the head of the corner. Neither is there salvation in any other: for there is none other name under heaven given among men, whereby we must be saved. – **Acts 4:10-12**ced*

The trap many men of God fall into today is trying to scratch the itching ears of this gospel saturated generation. Pastors spend far too much time trying to find cute poems and fascinating illustrations and far too little time rightly dividing the Word. The power of preaching has never been and will never be in the presentation or an outline. The power of preaching comes from a humbled servant who has reckoned himself dead in Christ and has yielded himself to be filled with the Holy Spirit and the Word of God.

You can speak as eloquently and intelligently as you want, but unless you've been alone with Jesus in the secret place of prayer, your preaching will be powerless. When Peter and John preached, they were the farthest thing from eloquent. Those who listened to them even noted from their delivery that they were *"unlearned and ignorant men."*

> *Now when they saw the boldness of Peter and John, and perceived that they were unlearned and ignorant men, they marvelled; and they took knowledge of them, that they had been with Jesus. – **Acts 4:13***

Their speech may not have been impressive, but one thing was certain: these men *"had been with Jesus."*

Brother pastor, teacher, or church leader is that the testimony of those in your congregation, class, or youth group? Can those who listen to you testify to the fact that they can tell you've been with Jesus when you speak? An awakened church is a church full of preachers, teachers, and laborers who deliver a clear message with a consistent biblical emphasis.

If God has given you the privilege of preaching or teaching his Word to others, I challenge you to examine yourself and your labor. Are your messages clear? Do they exalt and magnify Christ? Is your preaching or teaching saturated with the Word of God, calling out sin, and calling men to repentance in Christ? Prior to preaching or teaching, are you spending time alone with Christ? Are you satisfied with just getting a sermon or lesson together or are you seeking God's specific message for that day and that congregation?

If we reckon ourselves dead to self and alive unto Christ, there is no way that we can continue just throwing something together. The Holy Spirit is the Spirt of Truth, and He will guide us and lead us in our study and delivery if we'll rely on Him. The world has enough pulpiteers trying to impress the masses. What the world needs is some men of God who will boldly and plainly proclaim what the Lord says! May God help the message to be clear.

A Continual Increase

When the message is clear and God's people are filled with His Spirit, the end result will be a continual increase. Millions of dollars are spent every year by denominations and church strategists trying to find the magic solution to church growth. Some churches are convinced that all they need is a fresh young pastor to come in and appeal to the young folk. Others have thrown caution to the wind and have adopted every contemporary idea known to man to make their church not look, feel, or seem like a church. Many of the churches that have seen growth have seen lateral growth from other churches.

The growth that we desperately need is found in reaching the lost. In the early church, they continually saw souls saved and lives changed.

And they, continuing daily with one accord in the temple, and breaking bread from house to house, did eat their meat with gladness and singleness of heart, Praising God, and having favour with all the people. And the Lord added to the church daily such as should be saved. – ***Acts 2:46-47***

Chapter 9 – The Awakened Church

In the early church, seeing someone repent of their sins and follow Jesus wasn't a rare occurrence. Seeing someone saved in most churches today is as rare as a solar eclipse. This should not be so! Even worse, we've become so used to not seeing anyone saved that it doesn't bother us when we don't. We hardly ever hear someone ask a prayer request for someone to be saved. The list of those who are physically sick on our prayer lists is a long as a CVS Pharmacy receipt, but what about those who are spiritually sick with sin? A sin-sickness that, if untreated by the blood of Christ, will result in an eternity of unimaginable torment in Hell.

There is no clearer evidence that a church is spiritually asleep than the absence of a burden over the lost souls of men. A church that is awake is a church that is engaged in prayerful intercession on the behalf of the lost. It is a church that not only proclaims the great commission but practices it throughout their daily life.

An awakened church is never settled or satisfied with long seasons with no converts. We realize that every season in the church is not a harvesting season. There are seasons of preparation, planting, and purging, but there should also be a harvest. A church that is following Christ will always be more outwardly focused than inwardly focused. Christ's passion was the salvation of souls and as a church or Christian becomes more like Christ, they too will have a passion for souls.

Wholehearted Commitment

The average believer's commitment to Christ and the local church is downright shameful. Paul told the church at Rome that it was their *"reasonable service"* to live for Christ after all He's done for them. People, today, think if they give God an hour per week, then they're making a tremendous sacrifice. If they give God a dollar or serve in any capacity, then they act as if they're a spiritual giant. Yet everything in their life comes before God, and serving Him and attending church is something you do when you have nothing else better to do.

Sadly, this same attitude is held by far too many leaders in churches. If the average person attended work like they attend church, they'd be fired in a week. Vance Havner used to say, "A committee is a bunch of incompetents, established by the unwilling, to do the unnecessary."

Chapter 9 – The Awakened Church

What is even worse than such a church's lack of commitment is their attitude of entitlement. People who consistently miss weeks at a time of church will show up and speak out for twenty minutes at meetings and never flinch. Those same people are always offering up new ideas of bigger and better ministries that the church should be doing, and the majority of the time they won't show up if you have it.

Let me pause here for a moment and say, if you're that person, just stop! If you want to take weeks and even months away from church to do something that you deem is more important than serving Jesus Christ, then that is your choice and more power to you. However, when you do come back to church, come in, sit down, be quiet, and listen! Don't stroll in acting like you've just come down off the mountain with Jesus and you're ready to tell us all what to do. You're making a complete fool of yourself, and even though no one may be telling you so, they know it. God is more interested in your faithfulness than He is your frivolous ideas. I've never met a serious Christian who wasn't faithful to God's house.

An earmark of the awakened church is the absence of the uncommitted members. When

Jesus called Andrew and Peter, they forsook their nets and followed him.

> *"Now as he walked by the sea of Galilee, he saw Simon and Andrew his brother casting a net into the sea: for they were fishers. And Jesus said unto them, Come ye after me, and I will make you to become fishers of men. And straightway they forsook their nets, and followed him."* – ***Mark 1:16-18***

They wholly committed to following the person of Jesus Christ. Too many Christians today view salvation as a prayer or decision they made way back when, but they're not following Christ. Yes, there is a moment when we trust Christ, but salvation is not about reciting a prayer; it's about trusting in and following a person.

Modern day Christians don't want to forsake anything to follow Christ. They're not even willing to consistently forsake doing what they want for an hour or two a week to attend church. In an awakened church, there is no shortage of servants or laborers. It is a church where the

Chapter 9 – The Awakened Church

members get there early and stay late. It is a place they long to be and long to stay.

During the Welsh revival in the early 1900s, their prayer meetings would begin at seven o'clock and last until two or three in the morning. Some prayer meetings even lasted all night long. Those in an awakened church don't go to church to get out; they go to get in! Consider the testimony of those in the first church at Jerusalem.

"And all that believed were together, and had all things common; And sold their possessions and goods, and parted them to all men, as every man had need. And they, continuing daily with one accord in the temple, and breaking bread from house to house, did eat their meat with gladness and singleness of heart, Praising God, and having favour with all the people. And the Lord added to the church daily such as should be saved." – ***Acts 2:44-47***

Those early church members sold their possessions and put all they had toward the work of the Lord.

I'm not suggesting we sell our possessions, give away all our money, and go live at the church. God never asked them or us to do that. What I am saying is that they were sold-out and wholly committed to serve the Savior. They didn't withhold their tithes, their time, or their talents. Serving God wasn't a "Sunday" activity; it was a way of life. Daily they met at the temple and served the Lord.

Pastors today are fearful of scheduling a three-day revival because of the pitiful attendance it would have. The early believers met every day to worship and praise the Lord together. All of the problems we have with needing workers and servants in church would cease if the church would wake up! All the problems we have with empty pews and lousy attendance would end if the church would wake up!

As church leaders, we must recognize that the work that needs to be done in the lives of the uncommitted is a work in their heart. It is a work that only God can do. We can beg, plead, grovel, and try to shame people into serving, but if it takes all that, then those people shouldn't be serving anyway. Something is desperately wrong when you have to beg people to serve Jesus.

When the church is awakened from sleep, there will be more than enough committed laborers to see the work of God accomplished.

Providential Purging

Contrary to what many Christians believe, everyone who comes to your church shouldn't stay at your church forever. People come to churches for all kinds of reasons. Some come to grow in their faith and to have a closer relationship with Christ. Some come because they were raised that going to church was the right thing to do. Others come because they like to belong to social groups. Some come, especially in smaller churches, because they like power.

Beware of those in your church that long to be in positions of leadership. They are almost always going to cause trouble. People who think they should be in leadership usually should not be.

But in addition to all those people, there are others in the church that are placed there by the Devil to disrupt the work God wants to do.

> *Also of your own selves shall men arise, speaking perverse things, to draw away disciples after them. – **Acts 20:30***

One of the hardest things to accept as a believer is when someone, who you've attended church with for many years, becomes an enemy of Christ and the church.

The disciples dealt with that when they discovered Judas' betrayal of Christ. Often, it is not the enemy without that is destroying your church; it is the enemy within. It's not the atheist down the street, but the person sitting beside you in the pew. Satan will infiltrate a church with those who seem like the most sincere and wonderful people, and then when the time is right, he'll raise them up in an attempt to destroy the flock. Jesus taught about this same thing, and he used a powerful illustration about tares growing among the wheat to do it.

> *Another parable put he forth unto them, saying, The kingdom of heaven is likened unto a man which sowed good seed in his field: But while men slept, his enemy came and sowed tares among the wheat, and went his way. But when the blade was*

Chapter 9 – The Awakened Church

> *sprung up, and brought forth fruit, then appeared the tares also. So the servants of the householder came and said unto him, Sir, didst not thou sow good seed in thy field? from whence then hath it tares? He said unto them, An enemy hath done this. The servants said unto him, Wilt thou then that we go and gather them up? But he said, Nay; lest while ye gather up the tares, ye root up also the wheat with them. Let both grow together until the harvest: and in the time of harvest I will say to the reapers, Gather ye together first the tares, and bind them in bundles to burn them: but gather the wheat into my barn. –*
> ***Matthew 13:24-30***

Christ says that an enemy came and sowed tares amongst the wheat. The Devil is the enemy, and he has sown many tares throughout the churches in our land.

So, what does this have to do with providential purging? When a church is asleep, these Satanic spies typically go unnoticed. They subtly obtain more and more power and influence over the congregation. Some are well to do and others appear overly eager to help and serve. When the church is asleep and relying solely on the power of the flesh to guide their decisions, these spies thrive. They make wise decisions and choices that are just good ol' fashion common sense.

Remember, the Devil doesn't mind us being in church as long as we're doing it in the power of the flesh. However, if the church ever does begin to awaken, the true nature of the tares is revealed. They don't like the people following Christ and being led by the Spirit, because they want people to follow them. Like Satan prior to the fall, they want to be worshipped and refuse to follow God-appointed authority. When a church awakens, the members will stand together in unity as God exposes those who would deceive and destroy the flock.

We see a powerful example of how God purges the church from deceivers and hypocrites in the book of Acts:

And the multitude of them that believed were of one heart and of one soul: neither said any of them that ought of the things which he possessed was his own; but they had all things common. And with great power gave the apostles witness of the

Chapter 9 – The Awakened Church

> *resurrection of the Lord Jesus: and great grace was upon them all. Neither was there any among them that lacked: for as many as were possessors of lands or houses sold them, and brought the prices of the things that were sold, And laid them down at the apostles' feet: and distribution was made unto every man according as he had need.* – **Acts 4:32-35**

As we noted earlier in this chapter, people were selling their possessions and giving all they had to the church. This wasn't something the disciples prompted them to do; it was something they did willingly and joyfully.

Imagine being part of the early church and everyone around you gave all they had to the church. There would be a certain element of peer pressure to do the same. When we look at Acts 5, we see a husband and wife who wanted everyone to think they were sold-out to the Lord, but in reality, they were hypocrites:

> *But a certain man named Ananias, with Sapphira his wife, sold a possession, And kept back part of the price, his wife also being privy to it, and brought a certain*

part, and laid it at the apostles' feet. – Acts 5:1-2

Ananias and Sapphira had no obligation to give all they had to the apostles. This was a choice they made. The problem with what they did was that they kept back part of the money they received from selling their possessions, but made it appear that they were giving all they had made. It was deceitful and hypocritical to do so.

Yet, here is the dangerous part: how would anyone else know? It's no different than a man or woman appearing to be saved or appearing to pay their tithes. It may look like they're really sold-out, but God looks on the heart. God knew they were deceiving their brethren and that they would be a hinderance to the church. So, he revealed their sin to Peter:

But Peter said, Ananias, why hath Satan filled thine heart to lie to the Holy Ghost, and to keep back part of the price of the land? Whiles it remained, was it not thine own? and after it was sold, was it not in thine own power? why hast thou conceived this thing in thine heart? thou hast not lied unto men, but unto God. And

Chapter 9 – The Awakened Church

> *Ananias hearing these words fell down, and gave up the ghost: and great fear came on all them that heard these things.*
> *– Acts 5:3-5*

Because Peter was allowing the Holy Spirit of God to guide him and direct his life, he was sensitive to God's voice. God enlightened Peter to Ananias' scheme.

Even today, when a pastor is spiritually awake and walking with the Lord, God will give him insight about potential issues and obstacles that face the flock. How serious of an issue was this? So serious that God killed Ananias on the spot! He died right there in front of Peter and the rest of the people.

Unfortunately, the Devil rarely works alone. In this case, he used Ananias' wife as his cohort in crime. Often, it's a group of that person's friends or family members that serve as evil accomplices. Notice what happened to Ananias' wife as she acted out their deceptive plan just as they'd rehearsed:

> *And it was about the space of three hours after, when his wife, not knowing what was done, came in. And Peter answered*

> *unto her, Tell me whether ye sold the land for so much? And she said, Yea, for so much. Then Peter said unto her, How is it that ye have agreed together to tempt the Spirit of the Lord? behold, the feet of them which have buried thy husband are at the door, and shall carry thee out. Then fell she down straightway at his feet, and yielded up the ghost: and the young men came in, and found her dead, and, carrying her forth, buried her by her husband. And great fear came upon all the church, and upon as many as heard these things. – Acts 5:7-11*

She was just as guilty as he was, and she met the same fate that he had. Why would God respond so drastically? It was to purge the church of those who would choose to do it harm.

Notice that there was no uproar or mob of members rushing to Peter to dispute how unfairly their fellow members had been dealt with. No one called Peter an uncompassionate and unloving pharisee. This church was awake and being led by the Spirit. They were all in one mind and one accord, desiring the things of God.

I'm sure that none of them wanted to see Ananias and Sapphira perish, but they recognized that God's plan was more important than their feelings. No one likes to see people leave a church, but sometimes, it is what needs to happen for the work to move forward.

Many churches struggle for generations with powerbrokers or power clicks that run everything in the church. Nothing can be done without that individual's or that group's approval, and those people end up running most people off.

If the church awakens spiritually, God will purge the church of people and problems as He sees fit to allow it to grow. I'm not saying God is going to kill them on the spot, but He will remove the problem in a manner that allows the body to remain in unity.

Praise and Gladness

If there are two words that are overused in modern Christian circles it is the words "praise and worship." We talk a lot about praising God and worshipping God, but in many instances, that's all it is—talk.

When we attempt to worship and praise God in our flesh, it is boring and dull. The hymns are boring, the music is slow, and it is very unappealing. So, to counter the dullness, we've altered our music and style of worship to appeal to our flesh.

Let me pause here for a moment and say that this is not meant to be an inditement on contemporary music. Some contemporary music is powerful and has amazing lyrics that give evidence that God truly spoke to the songwriter. However, there is a lot of music that is written and performed in a manner that is directed at stirring up our flesh, but it does nothing for our spirit. When our flesh is stirred, our worship becomes synthetic and not authentic. The goal of worship is to be pleasing and acceptable to God, not man. When we sing and labor to be accepted by others, we have ceased from worshipping God to worshipping man.

Unfortunately, so many of the younger generations have never experience the power of being in a true Spirit-filled worship service. The result is that they cannot discern authentic worship from synthetic counterfeit worship. When a church is filled with people who have died to self and are allowing Christ to live through them, real praise and worship is experienced.

Chapter 9 – The Awakened Church

And they, continuing daily with one accord in the temple, and breaking bread from house to house, did eat their meat with gladness and singleness of heart, Praising God, and having favour with all the people. And the Lord added to the church daily such as should be saved. –
Acts 2:46-47

The early church experienced true worship and praise. They were filled with gladness and singleness of heart, and they worshipped God. They didn't have to rent out a coliseum and bring in a nationally known group to do it either.

When the people of God look to the cross and recognize who they are and what Christ did for them, they won't have to worry about praise! When the church is right with God, the result will be authentic praise and worship.

There are many things we could discuss in regard to the characteristics of an awakened church, but to sum it up, a church that is awake spiritually functions as it was designed to. The church becomes a place of unity and strength. It becomes a maternity ward for new converts, a spiritual college for disciples, and a hospital for the hurting. All the things we long for our churches to become turns into a reality.

I don't know about you, but I want to be a part of a church that has awoken to follow Christ. I want to pastor a church where the people are free to worship and are led by the Spirit of God.

What about you? What about the church you attend? Is it awake or asleep? If it's asleep, then it's time for you to get on your knees and begin to pray for God to send the wake-up call. It might time for you to rally some of the brethren together and begin to pray for God to break through. He's waiting if we're willing!

10

See the Fields

Say not ye, There are yet four months, and then cometh harvest? behold, I say unto you, Lift up your eyes, and look on the fields; for they are white already to harvest. – **John 4:35**

What are you going to do now? No matter whether you are a slumbering sinner or a snoozing saint, you can't plead ignorance any longer. You're accountable to that which you've read.

You may have been ignorant of your sleepy condition prior to reading this book, but not anymore. If you remain asleep in your sins or continue as a religious robot going through the motions as a saint, it will be in blatant disobedience to what God is trying to accomplish through this book. If you're lost, then you need to repent of your sins and ask Christ to save you. If you have been saved, then you need to leave off the traditions of men and allow Christ to live through you. So, I ask again, what are you going to do?

What you need to do is *"lift up your eyes, and look on the fields."* Some of our fields are like that of the slothful man Solomon spoke of in Proverbs 24. Other fields need to get back to the basics of sowing the seeds of the gospel instead of trying to create a modern-day seed that doesn't require the power of God and prayer to grow. No matter what your field may look like to you, Jesus says it is *"white already to harvest."*

That means there is a work to do now! There are people down the street, in your neighborhood, and in your community who need to be reached for Christ. Now that you're awake and your eyes are open, it's time you looked around and saw the great work that needs to be done right where you are.

God Is Able

Chapter 10 – See the Fields

Let's stop and address what your flesh and the Devil are whispering in your ear as you read. God is trying to encourage you, but Satan is trying to discredit God and discourage you about the work. The Devil is sowing thoughts of doubt and defeat. Perhaps you are already thinking that what I've written sounds good, but it simply isn't practical. Remember, Satan is trying to fill your mind with all the obstacles that might hinder you and your church from seeing souls saved and lives changed.

Perhaps you're concerned that you have an older congregation, or that you can't compete with the megachurch in town, or that you've already tried all of this before and had no luck. Maybe you're thinking that all this might work elsewhere, but it isn't practical in your town. Perhaps you're thinking that since your church is out in the country that much of this can't apply—after all, country folks are hard to reach.

All those excuses and thoughts might be true, but don't you think God knows all of those things too? Does the fact that it might be difficult excuse us from obeying God's command? Are the obstacles you face so great that God cannot overcome them? God forbid!

God is more than able, and He will make you able if you're willing to seek Him. If we find ourselves overcome by obstacles, it is evidence that we are looking through the eyes of our flesh and not the eyes of faith. We need to reckon ourselves dead in Christ and ask the Spirit of God to fill us and help us to see the victory we can have in Christ. Meditating on the obstacles and opposition we face will cause us to delay, postpone, and eventually neglect the harvest.

With all of that being said, I know where you're coming from. I too have found myself under the juniper tree, thinking all hope is lost. No matter how much faith we have in the Lord, the Christian life is full of peaks and valleys. There is not a man or woman that God ever used that wasn't well acquainted with the valley. However, sometimes it's not the valley; it's us. We are too often the problem. The disciples ran into this very problem while they were serving with Christ.

> *And when he came to his disciples, he saw a great multitude about them, and the scribes questioning with them. And straightway all the people, when they beheld him, were greatly amazed, and*

Chapter 10 – See the Fields

> *running to him saluted him. And he asked the scribes, What question ye with them? And one of the multitude answered and said, Master, I have brought unto thee my son, which hath a dumb spirit; And wheresoever he taketh him, he teareth him: and he foameth, and gnasheth with his teeth, and pineth away: and I spake to thy disciples that they should cast him out; and they could not.* – **Mark 9:14-18**

In those verses above, a man brings his possessed son to the disciples seeking help. The man's son was in very bad shape and had brought his family to the point of desperation.

As a pastor, I can't imagine a member of our church or someone in the community bringing their child to my office with the symptoms described in those verses. Even though it is overwhelming to think about for me, it was not uncommon for the disciples to face such situations.

Jesus had given the twelve disciples supernatural power to heal others and to cast out demons. This special gift would die out with the apostles, but it wasn't unusual for them to cast out demons. Yet, when they tried to cast out the demon in this man's son, they failed.

The father told Jesus, *"They could not."* The obvious question then becomes: why not? Why were they not able to cast out this particular evil spirit? It is not just a question you and I have; it's the exact question the disciples asked Jesus after He healed the man's son.

And when he was come into the house, his disciples asked him privately, Why could not we cast him out? And he said unto them, This kind can come forth by nothing, but by prayer and fasting. – ***Mark 9:28-29***

Once they were alone with Jesus the disciples asked Him, *"Why could not we cast him out?"* Was this a special kind of demon spirit? Did we say something wrong?

Jesus responded to them very plainly, *"This kind can come forth by nothing, but by prayer and fasting."* When Jesus spoke of "this kind," I don't believe He was speaking of the evil spirit but rather the power required to cast out the demonic spirit.

Chapter 10 – See the Fields

Jesus was saying that the only way to have the power to accomplish God's work was through our continued devotion to the Lord. This whole encounter was a lesson for the disciple's future. Their lack of power in that moment wasn't because they hadn't been fasting. Jesus told them there was no need to fast while He was with them. However, the day would soon come when Jesus wouldn't physically be with them, and in that day, they would need to live a life completely devoted to Christ if they were to have the power to see God do the impossible.

The point I'm trying to make is that God is able to help you see a great harvest right where you are. In spite of all the obstacles and difficulties, He is able! However, are we willing to fast and pray that we might have the power of God on our lives? We must move away from the idea that God only moves where all the pieces come together. You don't have to be in a thriving community, with a young vibrant minister, a talented energetic labor force, and wonderful media resources.

God can work in a place like that, or He can work in a one stoplight town with a seasoned minister, an older congregation, and next to no media. The ability to see God work does not rest in our abilities, but His! God is able!

God Is Needed

The world needs God! America needs God! I don't care who you are or what state you reside in, you are living on the mission field.

America used to be known for sending out missionaries, but now we are nation in need of missionaries. Our nation has forgotten where she came from and who made her great. God's people have sat on the sidelines quietly conforming for too long. We need to stand up and speak out about the godlessness taking place in our world.

The prominence of the Marxist and Socialist agendas are a direct result of God's people being asleep and unwilling to fight for truth. We need to stop drinking the tolerance Kool-Aid passed out by those who practice everything but tolerance. Tolerance to the ungodly means that you must tolerate everything they do without saying a word about it while they criticize, mock, and demean everything you do.

Fellow believers, it's time to open our eyes and see that our enemy has surrounded us. The Devil has infiltrated our public schools, our state funded universities, and our local and federal governments. They are either twisting and distorting the truth of God or they seek to wipe out Christianity altogether. If you don't believe that, consider what is being taught in many of our major universities across the country today. Many universities are now offering courses on "Queering the Bible." Below is a paragraph from a blog at smu.edu on queer bible hermeneutics:

> *Queer biblical hermeneutics is a way of looking at the sacred text through the eyes of queer people. It is important to understand the meaning of these terms in relation to the exegetical process. "Queer" is a term that collectively refers to people who are LGBT (lesbian, gay, bisexual, and transgender) and to people with fluid and non-binary genders and/or sexualities. Queer interpretations do not follow essentialist ways of defining gender or sexualities. A "hermeneutic" is "one's whole method of understanding or interpretation." Thus "queer biblical hermeneutics" is the approach, theory,*

> *and prospective that queer people use to understand the Bible.*

College professors and teachers across the country, who are paid with your tax dollars, mock, belittle, and discredit God's Word as mere fables and stories. Governors are more interested in fighting for the rights of pedophiles than they are the rights of churches to assemble.

During the COVID-19 pandemic, churches in California were fined thousands of dollars for exercising their constitutional right to assemble, while rioters, looters, and criminals were free to assemble without any opposition from the government. We could go on and on, but the point is, people need the Lord! All people need the Lord.

Even though so many of the ideologies and principles being promoted in our society, such as the cancel culture, gender fluidity, and the LGBTQ movement, are in clear contradiction to Scripture and are sinful, we should love them and seek to share the truth of Christ with them and others. I believe we need to take a firm stand on what is right and wrong, but we must also take that stand in love and remember the words of the apostle Paul:

Chapter 10 – See the Fields

Wherein in time past ye walked according to the course of this world, according to the prince of the power of the air, the spirit that now worketh in the children of disobedience. – **Ephesians 2:2**

God's people have no right to be arrogant in our stand against sin, because we too are sinners. However, now that we have seen the light of righteousness, we cannot condone darkness. We must speak the truth in love with a genuine desire to see others come to Christ. But we *must* speak! We need to cease from being silent and speak up about the ungodliness outside our doors. We need to follow Paul's example in Acts 17:

Now while Paul waited for them at Athens, his spirit was stirred in him, when he saw the city wholly given to idolatry. – ***Acts 17:16***

In this verse above, we see the Apostle Paul travelling to his next missionary endeavor. Paul had sent word to Silas and Timothy to meet him at Athens so they could travel together. In verse 16, Paul was waiting on Silas and Timothy to arrive. He most likely was thinking on where and how he'd try to reach those at his next destination.

His situation would be the equivalent to a person today sitting on a bench at the train station or in the airport. While he waited, he watched the people passing by. The longer he looked the more troubled he became until finally Scripture said, *"His spirit was stirred in him."* When Paul looked out at the people of Athens, he was troubled by what he saw, and it affected him. This is clear evidence that Paul was fully awake spiritually.

A child of God who can look out at a society consumed with carnality and wickedness without being stirred and troubled in their spirit is asleep. They've ceased to look through the eyes of faith and have chosen to view the world through the eyes of their flesh. When we view the world in our flesh, we are sympathetic to sin and sinful behavior because, deep down, we are still sinners.

We're like a dog that has been groomed, bathed, and smells wonderful who is looking out the window at a mutt across the street covered in dirt and licking up vomit. Deep down, the clean dog is a little jealous because it is in his nature to roll around in and dine on filth.

Chapter 10 – See the Fields

If we're going to see the fields the way Jesus instructed us to, we cannot look at the world through the eyes of our flesh but rather through the eyes of the Spirit. That's what caused Paul to be unexpectedly stirred at Athens. Paul saw that the people in Athens needed God, and it motivated him to do something about it:

*Therefore disputed he in the synagogue with the Jews, and with the devout persons, and in the market daily with them that met with him. – **Acts 17:17***

Paul didn't sit idly by, thinking it was too bad that Athens was so full of apostasy. No, he rose up and contended for the faith in the field of Athens. He disputed and challenged their idolatry and sinful lifestyle and beckoned them to know and turn to the true and living God. Notice that he didn't just go have a chat; he launched out with a daily campaign in the marketplace, trying to reach people for Christ.

He would eventually see his audience grow, and he had the opportunity to preach to large crowds at Athens. In true Pauline fashion, he didn't mince with words. He preached Christ crucified and risen from the dead. He told them about the appointed day of judgement when Christ would judge the world in righteousness. He didn't soft peddle it; he loaded up the ol' gospel gun and gave them both barrels!

That is the exact thing pastors, small group leaders, children's workers, and all Christians should be doing today. We need to stop dancing around the subject of the gospel. We must not be afraid to use words like sin, Hell, and judgment. It's no wonder people don't understand salvation in our churches. Unfortunately, we speak to sinners about their sin condition like a doctor who doesn't want to upset his patient by telling them they have terminal disease. We dance around the subject and try to avoid saying what needs to be said. We must, instead, clearly identify the sickness of sin so that we can share the good news of the true cure: the Son of God!

Now, I know what you're thinking. You're thinking that's all fine and good for Paul, but you're not Paul and not everyone is going to accept Christ when you talk to them about Jesus. Don't be deceived, Paul didn't see everyone come to Christ either:

And when they heard of the resurrection of the dead, some mocked: and others

> *said, We will hear thee again of this matter.* – **Acts 17:32**

There were those who mocked and scoffed at Paul. Just as many do today, they laughed the truth off as some foolish idea for wimps and sissies. Yet, there were others that received the message and wanted to know more. Paul didn't reach everyone at Athens, but some eventually gave their hearts to Christ:

> *Howbeit certain men clave unto him, and believed: among the which was Dionysius the Areopagite, and a woman named Damaris, and others with them.* – **Acts 17:34**

We cannot allow ourselves to abandon evangelism because some will oppose our message. Not everyone Christ preached to forsook their nets and followed Him. Christ knew that rejection would be an issue for His followers, so He told His own disciples plainly to move on when that happened:

> *And whosoever shall not receive you, nor hear you, when ye depart thence, shake off the dust under your feet for a testimony*

> *against them. Verily I say unto you, It shall be more tolerable for Sodom and Gomorrha in the day of judgment, than for that city.* – **Mark 6:11**
>
> *And whosoever shall not receive you, nor hear your words, when ye depart out of that house or city, shake off the dust of your feet.* – **Matthew 10:14**

When we're trying to reach people in our field and they reject us, we don't need to stop; we need to shake off the dust and move on because people need God.

Unfaithfulness Is Failure

All of us have a field to work in. Some fields are more glamourous than others, but no field is insignificant to God. You may be reading this book and thinking that you're a nobody, that you're only a church member in a small country church, or that you're simply a pastor of a few people and that the people down the street don't even know your name.

That's okay! Sure, we all want to be recognized as someone God is using mightily. We would all like to be thought of as a wonderful Christian and a sought-after pastor or teacher.

Chapter 10 – See the Fields

Yet, at the end of the day, we'll not be judged by how many people know our name. We'll not be judged by the size of our congregations, the titles we had, the positions we held in our associations, or by the conferences we spoke at. God is going to judge all of us by the same metric: were we faithful to our field? Did we faithfully plow in prayer and remove as many rocks and thorns as we could to make the soil as good as it could be? Did we give our best when we only had a few or did we give a half-hearted effort thinking it didn't matter?

Look, I know what it is like to preach to the wilderness of wood. I'm well acquainted with pouring my heart into hours of study, preparation, and prayer only to see a large portion of the congregation off playing instead of worshipping. It's not easy to stay faithful. There are many Monday mornings where pastors are overcome with thoughts of resigning, regrets, and reevaluating their life and ministry. Every pastor goes through seasons where they feel their labor is in vain.

It's not only pastors. I know many children's workers and small group leaders who labor and prepare all week and show up to near empty classrooms. These are not easy days to serve in a church, but we must never lose hope.

For to him that is joined to all the living there is hope: for a living dog is better than a dead lion. – **Ecclesiastes 9:4**

You may feel like the place you're called to serve is a dog of a place and that it's lacking in more areas than it's thriving. Yet, there is still hope because Christ is there in you. There is still work to be done. There are still souls to be saved and people to be reached for the Kingdom.

If God were truly through and there were no more souls to be saved and no more work to be done, then He would have already called us home. That day will come, but until that day, we are to be faithful to the work God has called us to do. I'm reminded of one of my favorite bluegrass gospel songs entitled, "Highway to Heaven."

The old preacher man stood there in the pulpit, The church house was empty almost; His eyes filled with tears, his mind filled with memories, Of not so long ago. When the church house was full, not

Chapter 10 – See the Fields

one pew was empty, The altar was stained with Saints' tears; As he stands there this morning and sounds out the warning; Once again letting them know.

(Chorus)

Verse 2:

Some of the members thought he was "old fashion", Unwilling to change with the times. So they found a new church with more modern day preachers, Who were willing to let things go by. But the old preacher stood for what he believed in, And what he had preached forty years; As he stands there this morning in a near empty church house, His opening remarks are these words:

(Chorus)

Verse 3:

Now the old preacher man stands there in that city; The city he's preached of so long. Oh, but he's never seen such a great congregation All gathered to welcome him home And he's never heard more beautiful singing, That is coming from that heavenly band. He's preached his sermon, He's carried his last burden. He's a rest in that heavenly land. But He'd still wants you to know.

Chorus:

There's a Heaven to gain, and a Hell to shun; The way is still straight, there's a race to be run. You can live as you please, but you must pay the cost; And the highway to Heaven still goes by the cross.

One day, we'll be in Heaven with Jesus, but until then, we must work the fields. As long as we're following Christ and working the fields, then we cannot fail. The only way we fail is if we fail to be faithful. If we fail to be faithful, then our churches, communities, cities, and our country has no hope. The next generations will have no chance at knowing Christ. There'll be no opportunity for revival or an awakening if we quit. Who knows whether or not God will send a great revival or awakening to your field, but if we fail to be faithful, we'll never know what He might have done.

> *Moreover it is required in stewards, that a man be found faithful.* – **1 Corinthians 4:2**

Our work is to let God do His work through us. That's not meant to be a copout or a license to be lazy. We are to diligently work in our field and do everything in our power to see people reached, but we are to recognize that God must give the increase. All our work is vain unless it has the blessing and anointing of God upon it.

Too often, we put pressure on ourselves that God never intended us to have. It's not your responsibility to build your class or your congregation; it's God's. He is the one who must provide the strength, the laborers, and the power to build as He sees fit. We are not in management; we're in sales and service. If we'll be faithful in sharing God's message and seeking to accomplish His will, then we will be successful.

You may never own a mansion, fly in a private jet, or have your face plastered on the cover of your new book on the shelves of

Walmart, but you will have the approval of the one who died to set you free. Popularity and worldly success don't impress God. He's not in awe of those ministers who draw large crowds and fill arenas.

Sadly, many Christians worship "successful" ministers and pastors like idols. They'll drive for hours, spend money on gas, hotels, and pay a fee to attend a conference where their idol is speaking. Meanwhile, they won't drive two miles on a Sunday to hear the man of God in their own church pour out his heart for free. In the eyes of God, success is measured by faithfulness and Christlikeness. So, dear Christian, don't be discouraged; just be faithful to what God has given you to do.

It's time to awaken from sleep and see the fields anew and afresh. It's time to remember that God is able and needed and that we have a responsibility to faithfully represent Him to this world. It's time to reckon ourselves dead so that Christ might live through us and empower us to be victorious in this world.

Are you awake? Do you know Christ as your Savior? If you do, then are you awake? Has your service to Christ become nothing more than a

Chapter 10 – See the Fields

mindless rut and routine of religious activity? If so, then it's time to change!

Get off the merry-go-round of apathetic Christianity and allow Christ to guide you and lead you where He would have you to go. Get out of the grave of religion and enjoy the blessings of your relationship in Christ.

Now that you're awake, it's time to help others around you awake. Take the things you've learned in this book and share them with others in your family, in your church, and in your community. May God help us to awaken to all God has for our lives!

About the Author

Scott Wilson accepted Christ as his Savior at the age of seven and was called into ministry at the age of seventeen. He is a native of Hickory, North Carolina. Scott has ministered in church all along the Southeastern United States and is a passionate pastor and preacher of the gospel. He has a true burden for the salvation of the lost and a desire to see revival in local churches and throughout America.

In addition to serving the Lord in full time ministry, he enjoys spending time with his wife Anne-Marie and their daughter Elisabeth Anne. Scott enjoys hunting, fishing, playing golf, and spending time with his family.

www.ingramcontent.com/pod-product-compliance
Lightning Source LLC
LaVergne TN
LVHW051517070426
835507LV00023B/3152